TRAVEL TIPS & TALES

WADDLE THE WORLD WITH RED PENGUIN BOOKS

Travel Tales & Tips

Lynn Aloia   Robert Intelisano
Stephanie Larkin

Janet Lipkin Bein ~ Lorraine Caputo ~ Carolyn Donnell
Joseph A. Farina ~ Gayle Lauradunn ~ Matt J. McGee
Terry A. Repak ~ William John Rostron ~ Jasmine Tritten
Larisa Veselova ~ Janet Metz Walter

Copyright © 2025

All rights reserved.

Published by Red Penguin Books

Bellerose Village, New York

ISBN

Digital 978-1-63777-739-8

Softcover 978-1-63777-740-4

No part of this book may be reproduced in any form or by any electronic or mechanical means, including information storage and retrieval systems, without written permission from the author, except for the use of brief quotations in a book review.

Contents

PART ONE
WHAT TO KNOW BEFORE YOU GO - BY LYNN ALOIA

1. INTRODUCTION — 3
2. PASSPORTS AND VISAS — 5
3. VACCINES — 12
4. TRAVEL ALERTS/WARNINGS — 15
5. BEFORE YOU LEAVE — 18
6. DAY OF TRAVEL — 21
7. EMERGENCIES — 23
8. APPAREL — 25
9. MONEY MATTERS — 28
10. LOCAL LAWS AND CUSTOMS — 30
11. SAFETY AND SECURITY — 33
12. MEDICAL — 37
13. PHONES AND ELECTRONICS — 39
14. DRIVING OVERSEES — 41
15. WORDS AND PHRASES TO KNOW — 44
    - Spanish: — 45
    - French — 46
    - Italian — 47
    - German — 48
16. CUSTOMS — 49

PART TWO
TRAVEL TIPS FROM ROBERT INTELISANO

1. SUMMER TRAVEL TIPS FROM ROBERT INTELISANO — 55
2. FALL TRAVEL, USE POINTS! — 61

PART THREE
TRAVEL TALES

1. TIME ALONG THE SILK ROAD—A HAIBUN	69
2. A SUMMER TRIP TO GRANNY	72
3. ADVENTURES WHILE DRIVING IN ENGLAND	76
4. MISSTEP ON A CATAMARAN IN COSTA RICA	79
5. BAD BEDS	83
6. NOT ALL THOSE WHO WANDER ARE LOST	86
7. CROSSING AMERICA BY TRAIN	89
8. UNEXPECTED GIFT	93
9. HOW TSA CAN SAVE YOUR LIFE	97
10. SOUTH-BOUND ON THE OAXAQUEÑO	102
Night	102
Morning	103
11. PERCORSO	105

PART FOUR
ITINERARY PLANNING

1. NARROWING DOWN THE CHOICES	111
2. TRANSPORTATION WORKSHEET	116
3. LODGING WORKSHEET	122
4. RESTAURANTS AND EXPERIENCES	127
5. PACKING AND LUGGAGE	131

PART FIVE
RECAP AND LESSONS LEARNED

1. REFLECTING ON YOUR TRIP	139
2. EATING AND DRINKING	142
3. TRANSPORTATION	146
4. ACTIVITIES	149

PART SIX
DAILY TRIP JOURNAL

30 DAYS OF MEMORIES	157
Meet Our Contributors	187
Also from the Red Penguin Travel Series	195

What to Know Before You Go

Expert Travel Tips by Lynn Aloia

Introduction

Once you have finalized your destination, the next crucial step is to gather a plethora of important details in order to ensure a smooth and well-prepared travel experience.

This section is your guide to most anything you need to know to keep your travels easy and enjoyable. Included are sections on:

- Passport and Card
- Visas
- Vaccines
- Travel Alerts and Warnings
- Before you Leave – Useful Suggestions
- Day of Travel – Useful Suggestions
- Emergencies
- Apparel

- Money Matters
- Local Laws and Customs
- Safety & Security Tips
- Food & Beverage Safety
- First Aid Kit
- Medical/Health Insurance
- Phones and Electronics
- Driving Overseas
- Words & Phases to know
- Customs – Declarations and Restrictions

Passports and Visas

Most U.S. citizens must have a U.S. passport to travel overseas and reenter the United States. This can be a passport book or the newer passport card. These are the only documents that are internationally recognized as valid, to identify you and your citizenship.

U.S. passports are issued only by the U.S. Department of State.

Passport vs. Passport Card vs. Enhanced Driver's Licenses (EDL)

The biggest difference between a traditional passport and passport card is that:

• Traditional passports are valid for **international travel** by **air, sea,** and **land.**

• Passport cards are valid only for **re-entering the U.S**. at land borders or sea ports-of-entry from:

Canada.

Mexico.

Bermuda.

The Caribbean.

Enhanced Driver's License (EDL)

• Is a driver license that resembles a passport card in that it identifies you as a U.S. citizen.

• Allows you to re-enter the U.S. from Canada, Mexico, Bermuda, and the Caribbean.

• Also like a passport card, an EDL is accepted only at land and sea border crossings—not for air travel.

Passports

First Time Application

To obtain a passport for the first time you will need to fill out the U.S. State Department's form DS-11. "Application for U.S. Passport." It can be found on the U.S. State Department's website and other passport agencies and acceptance facilities across the United States. The application form can be completed using the online form, but then must be printed and then signed in the presence of a passport acceptance agent. If completing it manually, use a black pen.

Proof of Citizenship

Proof of citizenship must be submitted with all passport applications. A previously issued passport; a certified, government-issued birth certificate; a consular report of birth abroad; a naturalization certificate or a certificate of citizenship can be used to prove citizenship.

Secondary documentation includes early public records, such as a hospital birth certificate or early school records, accompanied by a birth record, birth affidavit or a government-issued letter noting that no birth record can be found.

Proof of Identity

Proof of identity must be presented with all passport applications. Acceptable forms of identification include an existing passport, naturalization certificate, driver's license, military ID card or other current government-issued ID. A photocopy of the identity documents also must accompany the passport application.

A Passport Photograph

A single 2-by-2-inch passport photo must be submitted with each application. Passport photos must be in color and taken within the past six months in front of a white or off-white background. Applicants should look directly into the camera with a neutral expression and with the head taking up the majority of the frame.

Children under age 16*

All children traveling, including infants and newborns, must also have valid passports. For a minor under 16, the application process must be completed in person, and at least one parent must appear with the minor. You will need to:

• Fill out form DS-11

• Provide U.S. citizenship evidence for the child such as a birth certificate

• Provide parent's U.S. citizenship evidence

• Provide documentation showing parental relationship to the child

- Provide legal identification document of the parent such as a driver's license

- Provide a document of parental consent for the child to receive a passport

- Provide one passport size photo of the child

- Provide applicable fees

Some countries have instituted requirements to help prevent child abductions and may require travelers to present proof of relationship to the child/children and consent from any non-accompanying parent(s).

Minors Ages 16 and 17

Minors age 16 or 17 must appear in person at the time of application, and a parent or guardian must present some form of photo identification if the minor does not have one. This passport will be required for all international air travel with parents. The process is very similar for children under 16 years of age. The main difference is that it is possible to apply for the passport without a parent present. However, it is recommended that you provide a form of parental awareness such as a signed recognition consenting to the issuance of the passport.

When does your passport expire?

Adult passports and passports issued to persons at least 16 years of age are valid for exactly 10 years from the date of issue. Passports issued to children under the age of 16 are valid for 5 years from the exact issue date.

Can I renew an expired US passport?

If you have an expired passport, **you can renew it easily** by sending it in to the U.S. State Department, along with the required forms and payment. General processing time is 4-6 weeks. If you need your passport more quickly, you can also pay an additional fee to have the process expedited.

What does the Six Month passport validity rule mean?

The six month validity rule is imposed by foreign countries and not by the United States of America. It merely means that your passport should be valid for more than six months before you would be allowed to enter a foreign country that imposes the six-month rule.

Contact the embassy of your foreign destination for more information.

Traveling Outside the U.S. and Your Passport is Missing (Lost or Stolen)

File a police report immediately or at least within 24hours.

Find the nearest U.S. Embassy or Consulate and inform them of your situation.

Take with you:

• New Passport Pictures (taken before you go)

• Filled out Passport application

• Identification

• Evidence of U.S. citizenship

• Passport Fee

Keep in mind that most embassies and Consulates are closed on weekends and holidays, so you may have to adjust your travel plans. Remember you CANNOT cross international borders without a valid passport.

You may also be able to obtain an emergency passport. It will come within 24 hours, but it will only get you back to the U.S.

VISA

A Visa is a document that shows you are allowed to enter a country for a specify amount of time. Some countries require Visas while others don't. Country citizenship determines whether you need a Visa to enter a particular country. The U.S. state Department website list the countries that you are required to obtain a Visa.

Some Visas are required to be filled out before entertaining the country while others are granted when you enter the country.

The most common Visa types are:

• Work

• Student

• Transit

• Tourists

Visa applications can usually be found on the embassy or consulate website of the nation you want to visit. Print out the forms and fill them out. Find out the fee, which can run from $50.00 up to $250.00. and mail to the address provided. After your application has been processed your Visa will be mailed to you.

If you don't want to obtain the Visa yourself, there are agencies that can secure one for you. Keep in mind these fees can run up to $400.00 or more per Visa.

Replacing your Lost Visa

Your country's embassy or consulate cannot replace your Visa for you. You will need to visit the embassy of the country you are visiting to inquire about replacing an emergency exit Visa. You will need your passport or have to obtain an emergency replacement passport before you replace your Visa.

Passport Book vs. Passport Card vs. Enhanced Driver's License (EDL)

Document	Valid for Air Travel	Valid for Land/Sea Border Crossings	Accepted From
Passport Book	✓	✓	All countries
Passport Card	✗	✓	Canada, Mexico, Bermuda, Caribbean
Enhanced Driver's License (EDL)	✗	✓	Canada, Mexico, Bermuda, Caribbean

Vaccines

Many countries around the world have implemented vaccine requirements for travelers as a means to protect both their own population as well as incoming visitors. These requirements are typically based on public health considerations and aim to prevent the spread of diseases across borders. Vaccinations serve as a crucial tool in controlling infectious diseases, and mandating them for travelers helps ensure that preventable outbreaks are minimized. Such requirements usually focus on vaccinations against diseases that pose a high risk or are endemic in specific regions, such as yellow fever or polio. Travelers must provide proof of vaccination through an International Certificate of Vaccination or Prophylaxis (ICVP) commonly known as the "yellow card," which documents all necessary immunizations.

To find out the recommendations for the location you are planning to visit, check the U.S. Center of Disease Control (CDC) or the World Health Organization (WHO) sites.

If you do need vaccines, it is recommended you see your physician at least 6 weeks before you are scheduled to travel. It takes some vaccines 4 to 6 weeks to reach it highest protection. Additionally, not all vaccines are carried by all physicians, and you may need to visit a specialist or travel-health business in order to secure the necessary vaccines.

It is also suggested that some of the vaccines you received as a child be updated before traveling to high-risk areas. Check with your physician for their recommendations.

Here is a common list of vaccines you may need:

- Hepatitis A or hepatitis A immune globulin
- Hepatitis B
- Influenza (flu)
- Encephalitis
- Meningococcal meningitis
- Pneumococcal
- Polio
- Rabies
- Tetanus and diphtheria
- Typhoid Fever
- Varicella (chickenpox)
- Yellow Fever

Additionally, travel has been tremendously impacted by the COVID 19 epidemic, and many countries—as well as means of transportation—may have COVID 19 vaccination requirements in place. Find out early—preferably before travel arrangements are finalized—if vaccination requirements will impact your travel plans.

Travel Alerts/Warnings

Travel alerts and warnings are issued by the **U.S. Department of State** to inform travelers of **potential safety and security risks** in foreign countries. These advisories are designed to help U.S. citizens make informed decisions about international travel.

When a travel alert or warning is issued, **it is strongly recommended that you reconsider or postpone your travel plans** to the affected area.

Reasons for Travel Alerts or Warnings

The U.S. government may issue a travel alert or warning for a variety of reasons, including:

- **Civil unrest**
- **Terrorist activity or threats**
- **Outbreaks of disease or health emergencies**
- **Natural disasters (earthquakes, hurricanes, floods)**

- **Lack of U.S. diplomatic presence** (making it difficult to assist U.S. citizens in an emergency)

Each advisory outlines the specific concerns in the region and offers advice on whether travel should be avoided or approached with caution.

Stay Informed: Smart Traveler Enrollment Program (STEP)

The **Smart Traveler Enrollment Program (STEP)** is a free service provided by the U.S. State Department that allows U.S. citizens traveling abroad to:

- Receive **real-time alerts** about safety, health, and security updates

- Get important **travel advisories** specific to your destination

- Make it easier for the nearest **U.S. Embassy or Consulate** to locate and assist you in an emergency (natural disaster, civil unrest, family emergency, etc.)

Sign up for STEP at: https://step.state.gov

Embassy and Consulate Contact Information

Before you travel, **print out and carry** the contact details for the **nearest U.S. embassies and consulates** in your destination countries. In case of emergency, knowing where to go and how to reach consular officials can be critical.

Include in your travel documents:

- Address of the U.S. Embassy or Consulate

- Phone number and emergency contact lines

- Operating hours and local holidays

- Directions from your accommodation if possible

Where to Find Travel Advisories

To review the latest travel advisories, visit the official **U.S. Department of State website** at:

https://travel.state.gov

You can browse alerts by country, region, or threat level (e.g., "Level 4 – Do Not Travel"). Check this site **regularly** during the planning process and before departure, as conditions can change rapidly.

Being informed is the first step to being safe. Enroll in STEP, check advisories regularly, and plan your travels with confidence and caution.

Before You Leave

Following is a checklist to help you to remember all of the things to do/confirm before leaving on a trip:

☐ Let you neighbors know that you will be away.

☐ Contact post office to put hold on delivery.

☐ Set house light timers to turn on an off close to your regular schedule.

☐ Book a house sitter.

☐ Arrange for someone to water plants.

☐ Plan for the care of your pets or reserve boarding.

TRAVEL TALES & TIPS

☐ Cancel automatic deliveries, ie, pet food, newspapers, milk, mail.

☐ Refill prescription and buy any other necessary medications.

☐ Inform banks / credit cards companies you will be traveling.

☐ Notify you home alarm security company that you will be away. If the alarm goes off they will automatically, send the police.

☐ Turn off and unplug non-essential appliances from the wall.

☐ Check for guidelines of your airline or how many bags can be checked or carried on for free.

☐ Check to see what is covered by your homeowners or renters' insurance. Most policies cover up to a certain amount for items stolen away from home.

☐ Make photocopies of your itinerary and travel documents:

• Passport ID Page

• Visa

• Driver's License

• Birth Certificate

• Detailed itinerary

- Airline tickets
- Hotel reservations
- Credit cards
- Travelers checks serial numbers
- All confirmation numbers

Day of Travel

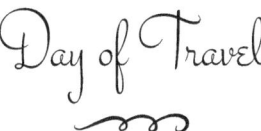

F ollowing is a checklist to help you to remember all of the things to do/confirm the day you are setting off:

☐ Pack an extra set of clothes in your carry-on bag, as your luggage could get lost.

☐ Take photos of all luggage in case of lost bags.

☐ If you are taking a taxi or other public transportation to the airport, be mindful of your conversation. Don't mention where you are going or how long your trip is. You could open yourself up for your house being robbed.

☐ If you are parking in long term parking, remove all sensitive information from your car – newspapers, magazines, mail that has your address on it. Remove your GPS and anything else of value.

☐ Bring snacks. Bringing snacks will hold you over until you can find a restaurant or food cart. Sometimes eating in a foreign country can be a chore.

☐ When you arrive at your hotel, take a business card from the front desk. If you get lost, you have the name and address in the local language.

Emergencies

No one wants an emergency to occur while traveling, but better prepared than regretful. Before leaving, confirm the following:

☐ You should have the contact information for the nearest U.S. embassy or consulate of the country you are traveling to. Personnel are available for emergency assistance 24 hours a day / 7 days a week.

☐ If your family needs to reach you, they can call the Office of Overseas Citizens Services in Washington, D.C. The State Department will relay the message to the officers on duty in the country where you are traveling. The consular personal will then try to locate you to pass on any urgent messages and, if necessary, report back to your family.

☐ If you or someone you are traveling with becomes seriously ill or injured, the local embassy or consulate can help in locating appropriate medical services and contacting your family. Personnel may also help in the transfer of funds from the U.S. Note, payment of hospital treatment and other expenses are your responsibility.

Apparel

Dress Smart, Travel Smart

The way you dress while traveling can say a lot about you—and it can have a significant impact on your safety and how you're perceived. Dressing appropriately shows respect for the culture you're visiting and can help you blend in, rather than stand out as a tourist. In some countries, inappropriate attire may not only be frowned upon but could also be against the law.

Dress with Cultural Sensitivity

Many countries around the world are more conservative than the U.S., especially when it comes to clothing. It's important to be aware of cultural norms and legal requirements before packing your suitcase. When in doubt, observe what the locals are wearing and follow their lead.

• Some religious sites—including churches, cathedrals, mosques, and temples—have **strict dress codes**.

• In some parts of the world, **modesty is expected**, especially for women. Revealing clothing such as **miniskirts, tank tops,** shorts, **capri pants, cleavage-baring tops**, and backless or sleeveless dresses may be inappropriate or even prohibited.

Footwear Matters

In many countries, **sneakers are reserved for sports activities**, and wearing them casually may mark you as a tourist. Instead, opt for **comfortable, closed-toe leather walking shoes** that offer support and blend in better.

What *Not* to Wear

Avoid clothing that may draw unwanted attention or cause offense:

- Items with **religious or military symbols**
- Clothing with **swear words or provocative images**
- Apparel featuring **national flags**, especially of foreign countries
- Garments with writing in **languages you don't understand** (you never know what it might say!)
- **Camouflage clothing**, which is illegal or restricted in some countries
- **Flashy prints or loud colors** that draw attention

Travel Apparel Tips

- Leave **flashy clothing, bags, and jewelry** at home
- Stick to **neutral colors** and **classic styles**
- Avoid **flamboyant patterns**

- Always **carry a lightweight scarf** – it can double as a head covering, shawl, or wrap when needed

Do Your Homework

Before you travel, **research the cultural and religious customs** of your destination. A little preparation goes a long way toward ensuring you dress appropriately and respectfully. When you look like you belong, you not only show courtesy—you may also reduce your chances of becoming a target for scammers or thieves.

Money Matters

Travel costs, and money matters are best to be considered long before they become money woes!

Before leaving:

Notify your bank and credit card holders that you are leaving and the dates you plan to be gone. This way they will not place a freeze on your account thinking it is being used fraudulently.

Check and understand the exchange rate of currency.

As you travel:

Avoid carrying large sums of cash with you. Use your credit cards.

Traveler's Checks — If you are using, only change them when you need them. These are not as popular as they once were.

Check ATMs for suspicious devices and cover your hand when entering your PIN number.

Never let you card out of your sight, and make sure it was only swiped once. If the transaction didn't go through, (unsuccessful or canceled), get a copy of the cancellation notice before attempting the transaction again.

If you've lost a card, have them stolen, or believe they may have been swiped or misused, contact your bank immediately.

Pay with credit cards at hotels and restaurants.

Insist on being billed in the foreign currency. If a merchant bills you in U.S. dollars, they can charge whatever exchange rate they want, often very high ones.

Local Laws and Customs

Respect, Awareness, and Responsibility

When you travel abroad, you are subject to the laws of the country you are visiting—not the laws of the United States. Being a U.S. citizen will not exempt you from local legal consequences. In fact, some actions that may seem minor or harmless in the U.S. can be considered serious offenses elsewhere.

Know the Law

Laws vary widely from country to country, and ignorance is not an acceptable defense. Before your trip, familiarize yourself with the legal system, rules, and penalties of your destination.

Examples of differences include:

- **Alcohol consumption** – Legal drinking age, public drinking, and alcohol availability vary widely

- **Dress codes** – Certain clothing may be required or prohibited, especially at religious sites

- **Photography restrictions** – It may be illegal to photograph government buildings, airports, or even local people without permission

- **Free speech limits** – Criticism of governments or religious beliefs may not be tolerated

- **Tipping expectations** – In some countries, tipping is standard; in others, it may be offensive

Be Aware of Local Holidays

Work weeks and national holidays may differ from what you're used to. For example:

- In many **Middle Eastern countries**, the work week runs from **Sunday through Thursday**

- During **religious or national holidays**, hotel and restaurant staffing may be limited, and services may be closed entirely

Plan accordingly to avoid disruptions.

Cultural Sensitivity Matters

Each country has its own set of customs and traditions. As a visitor, it's your responsibility to understand and respect them. Doing so not only shows courtesy—it also helps ensure a more enjoyable and safe experience.

Be especially mindful of:

- **Appropriate clothing** (e.g., headscarves, skirt/pant length, footwear)
- **Religious customs** and observances

- **Interpersonal behavior**, including gestures, touching, or displays of affection
- **Gift-giving etiquette**, punctuality, and where to sit in taxis or public spaces
- **Local attitudes toward food**, dining behavior, and tipping

Import and Export Restrictions

Just like the U.S. has customs rules, other countries enforce strict policies on what you can bring into or take out of their borders. Violating these rules may result in fines or legal trouble.

Common restricted items include:

- **Ivory or animal skins**
- **Religious artifacts or cultural relics**
- **Untreated wood products**
- **Antiques or historical items**
- **Jewelry or electronics** not declared upon entry
- **Precious or semi-precious stones**

Always check the specific **customs regulations** for each country you plan to visit.

Final Tip: Do Your Research

Every country has its own "dos and don'ts." Taking time to learn about them before your trip will not only help you stay out of trouble—it will also enhance your travel experience and open the door to more authentic cultural connections.

Safety and Security

You can never be too safe, especially when traveling to unfamiliar locations.

TIPS FOR YOUR SAFETY

Don't keep all of your money in the same place. When going out, take only what you think you will need. Secure the rest in your safe or safety box at your accommodations.

Don't carry your passport around with you all the time. Secure it in your safe or safety box at your accommodations. Of course, some countries may require you to have it with you at all times.

Keep your money / wallet in your front pocket.

Don't keep your wallet, purse, camera, or other valuables in your backpack.

Watch for "stall" tactics – thieves working in tandem. One will stop short in front of you while another will bump you from behind, giving them the opportunity to lift your wallet, take your camera bag, luggage, etc.

When in a position where your luggage will be separated from you, keep all your money and important documents on your person.

PACKABLE DEVICES:

Bug Detector — A device that can scan your room for hidden cameras and microphones.

Portable Door Lock — prevents the door from being pushed open, even if it has been unlocked, to help provide "additional safety, security, and privacy" while you are in, for example, your hotel room.

Portable Smoke & Carbon Monoxide Detector — A smoke alarm that tells you there's a fire nearby. A carbon monoxide detector or CO detector is a device that detects the presence of the carbon monoxide (CO) gas to prevent carbon monoxide poisoning.

Personal Alarm — A personal alarm is a small hand-held electronic device with the functionality to emit a loud siren-like alarming sound. It is activated either by a button, or a tag that, when pulled, sets the siren off.

AVOID SCAMS:

Do not use ATMs that are not attached to a bank.

Do not accept rides with a taxi driver whose meter is "broken."

Check the Federal Trade Commission website for other types of scams to watch out for.

FOOD AND BEVERAGE SAFETY

The safety of food and beverages, without strict public health standards, can never be guaranteed. Bacteria or parasites can go undetected causing illness in unprepared travelers.

The most common source of digestive problems while traveling, is water. You should avoid drinking the tap water and fountain drinks that is mixed with tap water. Also avoid ICE, even in mixed drinks, as it is also made with tap water. Drink bottled or can drinks that are factory sealed. You are better with carbonated drinks, such as soda or sparkling water, as the bubbles indicate a factory seal. Be cautious as some vendors may try to sell you tap water that is sealed with a drop of glue to mimic the factory seal.

You should also use bottled water to brush your teeth to avoid any contamination.

Avoid raw foods – Fresh salads, peeled vegetables, sauces made from fruit or vegetables should be avoided. The exception includes raw fruit and vegetables that you can wash and peel yourself.

Use caution with raw meats and seafoods, including foods cooked with any acid liquids.

Do not use unpasteurized dairy products, including cheese and yogurt.

Coffee and tea are best taken black unless you have pasteurized milk and dairy products from cold, factory-sealed bottles.

Avoid squeezed juice, fruit juice, ice pops, etc., made by others. It is fine to eat if <u>you</u> washed, cleaned, and squeezed the juice yourself.

Use precaution when consuming alcoholic beverages. The standard drink unit varies significantly from country to country.

It is usually safe to eat:

Foods served hot. High heat kills most of the germs.

Dry or packaged foods and food in factory-sealed containers.

Condiments such as mayonnaise, salad dressings, and ketchup that are in sealed packages.

Medical

When traveling, it is crucial to be prepared for personal medical needs to ensure a smooth and worry-free journey.

FIRST AID

Pack an ample supply of prescription medications and over-the-counter remedies for common ailments like headaches or upset stomachs. It is vital to carry these medications in your carry-on luggage as checked baggage may get lost or delayed.

Your personal first aid kit should consist of:

• Your prescription drugs in their original container. Some countries have strict restrictions on bringing medications into the country. Get a letter from your physician in case you are questioned.

• Pain medications – aspirin, ibuprofen, etc.

• Decongestants and antihistamines for allergies.

• Cough and cold medications.

- Medications for motion sickness.

- Antibiotic ointment, adhesive bandages, hydrocortisone cream, moleskin for blisters, sunscreen, and lip balm.

- Scissors, tweezers, nail clippers, thermometer, eye mask, ear plugs.

MEDICAL / HEALTH INSURANCE

Contact your insurance provider to find out if you are covered overseas. Some providers will cover the "customary and reasonable" hospital cost, but you may be required to pay for your care when you receive it.

If you do not have coverage overseas, you should consider purchasing a short-term policy that will cover you while you travel. Many travel agents and private companies can help you obtain International Travel Health Insurance for just a few dollars.

For your peace of mind you may also want to purchase Medical Evacuation Insurance. This will insure your transportation back to the U.S. if you become hospitalized.

NOTE — Social Security and Medicare DO NOT provide coverage outside of the U.S.

Phones and Electronics

When it comes to traveling, it is essential to plan ahead to ensure that your phone and other electronic devices work seamlessly throughout your journey.

Phone

One crucial aspect is checking the compatibility of your phone with the local networks in your destination country. Researching this beforehand allows you to determine whether you need to unlock your device or purchase a local SIM card for uninterrupted connectivity.

If available, you may simply activate your phone's global capabilities. Be aware that there may be a charge to do this. Many business travelers have an international data plan, but most infrequent travelers do not.

Additionally, familiarize yourself with different communication apps that offer internet-based calls and messaging, as they can save you from expensive international roaming charges while still allowing you to stay connected with colleagues, clients, or loved ones back home.

Electronics

Check the voltage of the country you are traveling to, as you may need adapters. In the U.S., your electronics run between 110-120 volts. A lot of overseas countries run at 220 volts.

Some devices have a switch that you can set to the appropriate voltage. Don't use a voltage adapter with a dual voltage device, as you run the chance of frying the device.

A converter or transformer may be needed to handle voltage compatibility issues. You may also need to get plug adapters as the plugs can be different shapes than in the U.S.

Consider carrying portable chargers or power banks to avoid running out of battery during long trips or when outlets are scarce.

Driving Oversees

Driving while traveling can indeed be a convenient mode of transportation for those who are well informed. Being knowledgeable about local traffic rules, road conditions, and the overall driving culture can significantly enhance one's experience on the road.

The best way to learn the road rules and laws of the country you plan to visit is to go to their government website.

Additionally, understanding local customs and etiquette helps foster positive interactions with other drivers and pedestrians during travel expeditions. By investing time in thorough research prior to embarking on a journey, individuals can confidently navigate unfamiliar roads as they explore new destinations with efficiency and ease.

Know the basics:

While the U.S. measure in miles, most of the world measures in kilometers.

To measure distance, approximately 0.6 miles is a kilometer, and 1.6 kilometers is equal to 1 mile.

The average speed on U.S. highways is 65 miles per hour. That converts to 105 kilometers per hour.

Things to consider before deciding to drive overseas:

Unfamiliar road signs

Price of gas

Driving on the opposite side of the road

Some roads may be narrow or even dirt

Driver's License:

Many countries do not recognize your U.S. Driver's license so you will need to obtain an International Driving Permit (IDP).

The only two ways to obtain one is through the American Automobile Association (AAA) or the American Automobile Touring Alliance (AATA). Any other sites that offer the IDP are not legit. Go to the website and print out the application. Fill out the application and send it with 2 original passport size photos, a copy of your U.S. driver's license, and the appropriate fee to the address they provide.

IDPs are issued to anyone over the age of 18 and has a valid driver's license and are usually valid for six months to one year.

Car Rental:

It is suggested that you book your rental before you travel to receive the best prices.

Insurance is mandatory. Check your auto insurance policy to see if you are covered for overseas car rentals. If so, you will need to carry proof of your coverage. If not, you will be required to take coverage from the rental agency.

If your plans include more than one country, ensure that your rental agreement allows for you to cross borders. It is usually allowed but there are some restrictions.

International Road Signs:

Colors and shapes can vary for international road signs, even from country to country. You should learn the basics of the country you plan to visit and have a printed version with you.

Basic road signs are divided into three categories: regulatory, warning, and informational or guide signs. Road signage will also include pavement markings, such as double yellow lines and crosswalks, and traffic signals, like train crossings and traffic lights

Danger warning signs are either triangles or diamonds depending on the countries. Restrictive or prohibitory signs are usually circular with red borders. Most signs have white or yellow background. A slash is used in most countries to prohibit something.

Words and Phrases to Know

You do not need to know the language of every country you intend to visit, but learning a few common phrases can help you as you visit. People will seem to help you more if they see you are making an effort.

There are also many translation apps you can download to help with communication.

Some everyday phases to learn:

Hello

Goodbye

Thank You

Please

My name is

Do you speak English?

Where is the bathroom?

How much?

The numbers 1 – 20.

Here they are in some of the more common travel languages:

SPANISH:

Hello   *Hola*

Goodbye   *Adiós*

Thank You   *Gracias*

Please   *Por favor*

My name is   *Mi nombre es*

Do you speak English?   *¿Hablas inglés?*

Where is the bathroom?   *¿Dónde está el baño?*

How much?   *¿Cuánto cuesta?*

The numbers 1 – 10   *Los números 1 – 10*

1 - uno

2 - dos

3 - tres

4 - cuatro

5 - cinco

6 - seis

7 - siete

8 - ocho

9 - nueve

10 - diez

FRENCH

Hello   **Bonjour**

Goodbye   **Au revoir**

Thank You   **Merci**

Please   **S'il vous plaît**

My name is   **Mon nom est**

Do you speak English?   **Parlesz-vous anglais?**

Where is the bathroom?   **Où se trouvent les toilettes?**

How much?   **Combien?**

The numbers 1 – 10   **Les chiffres de 1 à 10**

1 - un

2 - deux

3 - trois

4 - quatre

5 - cinq

6 - six

7 - sept

8 - huit

9 - neuf

10 - dix

ITALIAN

Hello   *Ciao*

Goodbye   *Arrivederci*

Thank You   *Grazie*

Please   *Per favore*

My name is   *Mi chiamo*

Do you speak English?   *Lei Carla ingress?*

Where is the bathroom?   *Dov'è il bagno?*

How much?   *Quanto?*

The numbers 1 – 10   *I numeri 1 – 10*

1 - uno

2 - due

3 - tre

4 - quattro

5 - cinque

6 - sei

7 - sette

8 - otto

9 - nove

10 - dieci

GERMAN

Hello **Hallo**

Goodbye **Auf Wiedersehen**

Thank You **Danke**

Please **Bitte**

My name is **Ich heiße**

Do you speak English? **Sprechen Sie Englisch?**

Where is the bathroom? **Wo ist die Toilette?**

How much? **Wie viel?**

The numbers 1 – 20 **Die Zahlen 1 – 20**

1 - eins

2 - zwei

3 - drei

4 - vier

5 - fünf

6 - echs

7 - sieben

8 - acht

9 - neun

10 - zehn

Customs

There are customs—like the different traditions and ways of doing things around the world, and then there is Customs—or the rules regarding what you may bring back with you after a trip. This section will focus on the latter.

DECLARATIONS AND RESTRICTIONS

When returning to the U.S., there are items that must be "declared" at customs. This is for anything you purchase abroad, in a duty-free shop, on board a boat or on an airplane. You will do this on the Custom and Border Protection form provided to you. You will list the cost of each, including taxes for:

- Item you purchase for yourself.

- Items / Gifts you purchased for others

- Items you inherited

- Items you brought intending to sell or use in your business.

If you don't know the cost of an item, estimate its fair retail value in the country that you received it.

There are exceptions for what and how much you can bring into the U.S.

*Customs Duty is a tariff or tax imposed on goods when transported across international borders. The purpose of Customs Duty is to protect each country's economy, residents, jobs, environment, etc., by controlling the flow of goods, especially restrictive and prohibited goods, into and out of the country.

*Duty-free shops (or stores) are retail outlets that are exempt from the payment of certain local or national taxes and duties, on the requirement that the goods sold will be sold to travelers who will take them out of the country.

Duty-Free Exemption

The duty-free exemption, also called the personal exemption, is the total value of merchandise you may bring back to the United States without having to pay duty. You may bring back more than your exemption, but you will have to pay duty on it. In most cases, the personal exemption is $800, but there are some exceptions to this rule. There are some limits on the number of alcoholic beverages, cigarettes, cigars, and other tobacco products you may include in your duty-free personal exemption.

Restricted Items

Restricted means that special licenses or permits are required from a federal agency before the item is allowed to enter the U. S.

Examples of restricted items include firearms, certain fruits and vegetables, animal products, animal by products, and some animals.

Prohibited Items

Prohibited means the item is forbidden by law to enter the United States.

Examples of prohibited items are dangerous toys, cars that don't protect their occupants in a crash, bush meat, or illegal substances like absinthe and Rohypnol.

Before you bring anything back with you to the U.S., check the website of the Homeland security to find out the requirements.

Website of the U.S. Department of Homeland Security: https://www.dhs.gov/

Travel Tips

from Robert Intelisano

Summer Travel Tips from Robert Intelisano

There is a saying amongst planners that the average person spends more time planning a 2-week family vacation than they do planning their own retirement! While the average person should spend more time planning retirement, the planning time for your 2-week family vacation is justified for several reasons.

As per the NY-1 interview of Robert Sinclair Jr., Senior Manager of Public Affairs at AAA (Automobile Association of America,) 2022 had some of the worst flight delays and cancellations in history! The lack of travel followed by huge demand increases, left airlines short-staffed and scrambling to hire and rehire personnel.

Also, due to retirements and attrition, there is a national shortage of Air Traffic Controllers. "In 2022, 70% of ALL weather-related delays in the USA stemmed from New York's 6 airports (includes Newark, MacArthur, Westchester and Teterboro Airports) because of the connecting hub and spoke system," said Mr. Sinclair.

Here are my updated TOP 10 Summer Travel Tips:

1. Book Flights Early: Air fares are up 40% from last summer and there are projections for more increases; hence, now is a good time to book flights and secure your trip. Also, there is a 250% increase in international bookings, so try and book those now as well. Many countries, such as Japan and China, have lifted Covid restrictions.

2. Call Your Credit Card Company in Advance: Give them your full itinerary, with dates in each city. I have had credit cards frozen after the credit card company had seen a string of out-of-town expenditures.

3. When Packing Start from Feet to Head: This is a good thing to do in the morning getting ready for work. I start from feet to head and pack in piles.

4. Pack a Change of Clothes in your Carry-on Bag: Over 29 million bags are lost or delayed each year. Be ready when and if it happens to you.

5. Buy an Off-Color Suitcase: This decreases confusion and is more easily recognizable during ground-transportation madness when people are jockeying for their luggage.

6. Sign Up for the TSA: The TSA pre-check can make the difference between making and missing a flight. It offers better distancing and eliminates the need to remove shoes, belts and/or laptops expediting the process. TSA memberships cost only $85 and are valid for 5 years. The renewal is discounted to $70 if done online at tsa.gov/precheck.com, or $85 in person.

7. Research AAA and Airline Vacation Packages: It is no secret that airlines and hotels have been hurt by the pandemic. There are some sweet short-notice vacation packages available right now. Check out AAA.com, JetBlueVacations.com and

AAvacations.com to name a few, and **save big money**! If you have points with your preferred airline, start with them.

8. Read Both Positive and Negative Hotel Reviews: Try booking.com, tripadvisor.com and kayak.com for domestic travel. For same-day rooms use **hoteltonight.com.** It is a money-saving, excellent FREE APP to download onto your smart-phone to **save big $$$.**

9. If Driving, Schedule a Tune-up, and Map Your Journey in Advance: A good way to avoid getting into a spat with a spouse or loved one, lol. There is nothing worse than a car breaking down or getting lost on a road trip. My preference is WAZE over Google Maps. WAZE (owned by Google) downloads faster and has an information sharing agreement with over 800 US cities and international countries. Waze also warns you about upcoming speed traps, red-light cameras, and debris on the road.

10. Try to NOT Check Bags: Not if, when flights get changed or cancelled last minute, it is much easier to adapt when you don't have to retrieve your checked bag.

11. Call Alternate Phone Numbers: If you get stuck at the airport because of a cancelled or changed flight, everyone rushes to the gate or calls the general phone number. **The smart move is to buck the trend and call the airline rewards number and/or international number to change your flights!**

12. Consider Using a Professional Travel Agent: Covid-19 has weeded out many of the weak travel agents. There are hotels that share their room booking commissions with the travel agent, so it does not always mean more money out of your pocket. Also, most travel agents have access to "The Apollo System" which allows them to access multiple airline sites at the same time, which makes it easier to rebook your flights and save money.

I have spoken with family friends who haven't been away since covid-19, and some say they are a little rusty regarding travel. Sometimes people put too much pressure on themselves to have a good time in this situation. Planning in advance can help ensure a smoother summer vacation. Have a fabulous trip and enjoy your summer!

My 6 Tips to SAVE Money on Travel:

1. **Research AAA and Airline Vacation Packages:** Airlines and Hotels must make up for lost profits, so deals can be had with both advanced and short notice. **Search aaa.com, jetbluevacations.com and aavacations.com to name a few and save money on vacation packages.**

2. **Bring Your Own Food in Ziplock Bags:** Not only is this safer, it saves money on overpriced airport fast food and buying those awful "meal boxes" most airlines are now selling by credit card only on board. Most airlines have eliminated meals (there was no meal offered on my 5-hour San Diego to JFK flight last Sunday).

3. **Input Your Hotel and Flight Itinerary Dates in Advance:** If you know your travel dates in advance, there are several websites you can input your dates in advance, that will track pricing and email you automatically when they decrease. I like airfarewatchdog.com for flights and there are many hotel options like kayak.com, hotels.com and booking.com.

4. **Consider Checking One-Way Flights After Checking Round Trip Options:** This strategy can be effective, especially if you are pigeon-holed into traveling during school breaks when airlines notoriously prop up fares. I saved over $150 by booking 2 one-way tickets on my California trip. New Yorkers have a built-in advantage by having multiple airports so you might fly out of LaGuardia and back into JFK airport, which is what I just did.

5. **Consider Alaska Air Especially to the West Coast:** Alaska Air has a new partnership with American Airlines (the largest USA airline) and they have joined the One World Network. Alaska offers non-stop flights from Kennedy Airport to Los Angeles, San Francisco, Seattle, Portland, and San Jose. Non-stop Alaska Air flights from Newark Airport to San Diego, LA, San Francisco, Seattle, Portland, and San Jose. Alaska Air have no designated LaGuardia terminal; however, they do offer codeshare flights on other airlines. **Alaska rates are usually lower than the bigger carriers and points are still available on American Airlines by flying Alaska Air!**

6. **Download the Hotel Tonight Free App on Your Smart Phone:** Many people are unaware that you can get excellent hotel rates by waiting until the same day of travel. This is not for everyone! In a unique situation, I found out there was a nursing convention the weekend I had to be in Santa Barbara. Rates were almost double that weekend with 2-star hotels getting over $250/night. I decided to take my own advice and opened the Hotel Tonight App (they use GPS) as soon as I landed at 8p that night. Low and behold I found a 3-star hotel for 2 nights, less than what the 2 stars were charging. Hotels would rather fill a room last-minute for less profit than earning $0 with an open room.

My 4 Tips for a Quality Trip Are:

1. **Consider Signing Up for the TSA Pre-Check:** In April 2021, 98% of TSA Pre-Check passengers waited less than 5 minutes as per www.TSA.gov/precheck. It takes 5 minutes to complete an online application and schedule a 10-minute in-person appointment that includes a background check and electronic fingerprinting at an enrollment center. The $85 fee is good for 5 years.

2. Consider Buying an Off Color or Design Suitcase: There are 20 million bags lost per year, most of them are black! An off color or funky design sets your bags apart and makes them easier to spot from a long distance.

3. Read Negative Hotel Reviews First: I like tripadvisor.com best for this. Better to put in the time upfront instead of checking into a grimy hotel that looks different from their online pictures. If this happens, refer to my money saving Tip #6 and change hotels immediately!

4. Consider Using a Professional Travel Agent: Covid-19 has weeded out many of the weak travel agents. There are hotels that share their room booking commissions with the travel agent, so it does not always mean more money out of your pocket.

For my Financial Wave readers, feel free to reach out to me at Rob@InsuranceDoctor.us for more information or a travel agent referral.

Fall Travel, USE Points!

With cooler temperatures, smaller crowds, and more laid-back vibes, the fall provides a welcome respite from the hectic summer pace.

And since the weather can be more variable and fewer people are venturing far from home, it also tends to be a great time to score deals on flights and lodging. As you're sorting out how to maximize your PTO (Paid Time Off) for the rest of the year, consider saving big $$$ by using points.

Some issues with using points, whether it is airline, credit card or hotel points, is that it is confusing and also like trying to hit a moving target as companies are constantly changing their points programs. Usually, these changes result in points being less valuable.

This is where "The Points Guy" comes in! They have created formulae to convert points into dollars and cents and vice versa. If you have an I-phone, feel free to go to the app store and download "The Points Guy" app. Currently, there is no "Points Guy" app for androids, so you can use the charts below.

Reasons to book fall travel NOW:

1. Lower Prices: Travel demand plummets as kids go back to school!

2. Better Deals: Airlines and hotels know fall demand is lower, so they sweeten their offers for cash and points pricing.

3. Holidays: There are two schools of thought: Work around the holidays, or take your vacation overlapping with a holiday to use less Paid Time Off days.

4. Points, Points, Points: The fall is the best time to cash out on points (before their values go lower) and recently, two major airlines have revamped their FF (frequent flyer) programs.

NOW is the time to check your points and consider flushing them out, see the charts below, which list cents per mile and bon voyage!!

TRAVEL TALES & TIPS

Credit Card Rewards Programs

Program	Value (¢/pt)	Latest News
American Express Membership Rewards	2.0	Effective April 1, 2025, REI Gift Cards are no longer available for redemption in the Membership Rewards program. Additionally, significant changes to credit card terms and benefits, including how users earn and redeem reward points, will take effect in June 2025.
Bilt Rewards	2.05	Introduced new initiatives allowing members to use rewards points to pay off student loans through providers like Nelnet, MOHELA, and Sallie Mae. Also, offered a one-day transfer bonus to Southwest Airlines on May 1, 2025, with bonuses ranging from 25% to 100% based on elite status.
Capital One Miles	1.85	Opened a new Capital One Lounge at Washington D.C.'s Dulles International Airport (IAD). Additionally, clarified application restrictions with a new 48-month rule and launched a new Lifestyle Collection of hotels.
Chase Ultimate Rewards	2.05	Launched "25 Trips to Take in 2025" campaign, giving away one million Chase Ultimate Rewards points to ten eligible cardmembers. Continues to offer 1:1 point transfers to 14 loyalty programs.
Citi ThankYou Rewards	1.8	Announced a reduction in the transfer rate to Emirates Skywards from 1:1 to 1:0.8, effective July 27, 2025. Additionally, Citi is phasing out its Rewards+ credit card and replacing it with the new Strata Card, available in summer 2025.

Airline Loyalty Programs

Program	Value (¢/mi)	Latest News
Air Canada Aeroplan	1.5	Offering up to 40,000 bonus points with the TD® Aeroplan® Visa Infinite* Card for applications approved by June 3, 2025. Additionally, the Chase Aeroplan Credit Card is offering 75,000 bonus points after spending $4,000.
Alaska Airlines Mileage Plan	1.4	Enhanced Mileage Plan loyalty program with personalized rewards, including bonus miles, upgrades, and lounge access. Cardholders will earn one elite-qualifying mile for every $3 spent on qualified purchases, up to 30,000 EQMs.
American Airlines AAdvantage	1.5	AAdvantage members can now use miles for inflight food and drink, as well as American Airlines Cruises sailings. Additionally, AAdvantage Credit Cardmembers can earn 2 miles per $1 spent on select cruise bookings.
All Nippon Airways Mileage Club	1.4	No recent updates available.
Asia Miles	1.3	No recent updates available.
Avianca LifeMiles	1.7	No recent updates available.
Avios (British Airways)	1.5	British Airways rebranded its Executive Club to the British Airways Club and revised its tier points system, making it harder to retain elite status.
Delta Air Lines SkyMiles	1.2	Implemented a "lounge meter" starting February 1, 2025, limiting American Express premium cardholders to 10 or 15 visits annually, with each extra visit costing $50.
Emirates Skywards	1.2	Restricted first-class award ticket availability exclusively to elite members—Platinum, Gold, and Silver—effective May 12, 2025.

TRAVEL TALES & TIPS

Etihad Airways Guest	1.2	Introduced a complimentary Abu Dhabi pass for its passengers, including a tourist SIM card with 10GB data and unlimited access to public buses.
Flying Blue (Air France/KLM)	1.2	Launched new Promo Rewards with flights to Europe from just 11,250 miles.
Frontier Airlines Miles	1.1	No recent updates available.
Hawaiian Airlines HawaiianMiles	0.9	No recent updates available.
JetBlue TrueBlue	1.4	Began service to Amsterdam Airport Schiphol (AMS).
Korean Air SkyPass	1.7	No recent updates available.
Singapore Airlines KrisFlyer	1.3	No recent updates available.
Southwest Airlines Rapid Rewards	1.4	Offered a limited-time Companion Pass promotion, now expired.
Spirit Airlines Free Spirit	1.1	No recent updates available.
Turkish Airlines Miles&Smiles	1.3	No recent updates available.
United Airlines MileagePlus	1.45	Launched an award sale to South Pacific destinations.
Virgin Atlantic Flying Club	1.5	No recent updates available.

Hotel Loyalty Programs

Program	Value (¢/pt)	Latest News
Accor Live Limitless	2.0	No recent updates available.
Best Western Rewards	0.6	No recent updates available.
Choice Privileges	0.6	Launched college football experiences, selling out in less than 12 hours.
Hilton Honors	0.6	No recent updates available.
IHG One Rewards	0.5	Announced new brand (Garner) for budget travelers.
Marriott Bonvoy	0.84	Launched a limited-time offer on cobranded business card.
World of Hyatt	1.7	Began disclosing resort fees in daily rates and launched a limited-time offer on cobranded business card.
Wyndham Rewards	1.1	No recent updates available.

Travel Tales

Stories from Around the Globe

Time Along the Silk Road—a Haibun

GAYLE LAURADUNN

In Samarkand dwells Furkat, his wife, and four intelligent, beautiful daughters, ages 23-13. Their parents make them citizens of the world and the family speaks only English at home. The daughters also know Chinese, French, and Japanese. These young women are eager to stride the globe. The evening we guests from afar sit at dinner with the family, Furkat rises, hoists his glass and announces the eldest is to be married. We chorus our congratulations to her blushes.

Allah beguiles

dare climb seven empty steps

stairway to nowhere

Around the long table laden with many more delicious dishes than we can consume—all prepared by the second eldest—chatter erupts about the prospective groom. Who is he? What is his work? We tease her if he is handsome, tall or short, and if he speaks many languages. She blushes the more and giggles at our impertinence.

commerce carves silk road

Buddha graces—

maelstrom of faith wars

She responds she has never met him. In Uzbek tradition, marriages are arranged.Like that of her parents. Like that of everyone she knows. This dinner is also a celebration of her parents' 27th wedding anniversary. The daughters have decorated the dining room. Balloons and streamers color the walls, the ceiling, the very air.

silk beckons

traders respond

two-hump camels travel wide

Her mother says the arrangements are not final. The groom's parents request the girl follow custom and spend 40 days in their home before the wedding. Even though it has been explained to them, if she does this, she will lose her job. Her employer allows only two weeks vacation time. With reluctance his parents agree. The public health agency for which she trains organizations local and abroad in improved methods treats her well. She speaks eight languages fluently and has lived and worked in Japan, Germany, Italy and other countries for months at a time.

long road links east to west

Nukus, Bukhara, Tashkent

Samarkand glows

After this exciting announcement, she reads a letter to us she received that day. Johns Hopkins University invites her to attend a six-week training in Baltimore on a new program they have developed. She is thrilled. We guests from afar applaud loudly. Then Furkat tells us the groom is a policeman. Silence reigns around the table. The two youngest giggle and offer to read to us in Chinese.

marry a stranger

stay hidden at home

marry languages

Two days later, in our bus to Tashkent, Furkat receives a call from his wife: the groom's parents have called off negotiations for the marriage because "the girl refused" to spend the 40 days with them.

far-away stretches beyond

black and white on beige sand

magpies

A Summer Trip to Granny

LARISA VESELOVA

In the summer of 1959, our family traveled from Ukraine to the Urals, our mother's homeland. Maybe we had been there before, but that trip I had remembered most vividly. Probably, it also was connected with our Dad's interest in photography at that time, so, later we had the opportunity to look at the photographs of this family trip and refresh our feelings.

We traveled from the town of Nizhin in Chernihiv area in Ukraine to the village of Big Balandino in Chelyabinsk region for three long days by train with a transfer in Moscow. Everything was incredibly interesting for us (three kids of nine, seven and five) - to ride in a couchette car, to move from the bottom shelf to the top shelf and back, to drink hot tea from glasses with metal cupholders and pieces of sugar inside them that melted before our eyes. That tea was brought by the conductor of our carriage three times a day. We could enjoy the changes of landscape through the train window. We also liked getting off to the platform of the large stations and counting the number of freight cars in the coming trains...

On the second day of our trip, when the train was crossing the Volga River, we rushed together to the exit to look at the greatest

Russian river. Our brother Nick was a preschooler and could not run fast. One of the children slammed the iron door in front of him, not seeing that the child had already put his fingers in the doorway...

Nick screamed in pain! We were afraid that he wouldn't be able to move his fingers - they became blue and lifeless... Remaining part of the way we carried him cold water so he could keep his fingers colder (there was no ice in the carriage that time at all).

When we arrived to Big Balandino, our family was greeted by many cousins.

Mother's older sister, Aunt Eudokiya (or Dunya in short way) and her husband Nazar had five children: Mariya (Masha), Alexandra (Shura), Anna (Nyura), Pavel (Pasha) and Michael (Misha). When we came into their small wooden house, Aunt Dunya asked if any of us could go to their garden and pick some cucumbers. We were kids raised in the town and did not know how to do this. Our brother Nick grabbed a large cucumber and pulled on it, but he took out all the wine with several cucumbers on it. Aunt Dunya was very surprised:

"Wow, those town kids don't know how to pick a cucumber!"

I watched some icons for the first time in my life and they were very strange to me.

Another Mom's sister, Aunt Sofiya, had an adult son, Pavel (he was called by a name incomprehensible to me - Punka) and ten-year-old daughter Nellie. They all lived with grandmother Anfissa in the same small wooden house where our mother was born. Food still cooked in a large Russian oven, on the side of which you could climb on the stove and bask on the couch. Luckily, a year before the house became bigger - a second room was attached to it. Our family of five stayed in their house for three weeks, and we felt love and comfort.

Pavel, son of Aunt Sofiya, was stocky and sturdy. He was the only blonde person in the family, with whitish eyelashes, and it seemed to us awesome. He worked first at a marble quarry in the nearby Prokhorovsky village. Then he was trained as a chauffeur. His open three-ton car went to the state farm where his family lived during the Second World War.

We also met Alexander, son of deceased Aunt Anna. I always called him "Uncle Sasha" - he was seventeen years older than me, and my tongue did not turn to call him another way.

We liked life in the village very much! We ran to swim in the pond, we went to the woods to gather berries. The strawberries were small, but sweet, the drupe was rare. Later, trips for mushrooms began: the loads were white and gray, the chanterelles were bright red, rawhides were multicolored- everything looked so beautiful! During that summer when we learned to distinguish between edible and poisonous mushrooms (maybe that's why they are still alive and have never been poisoned by mushrooms). The basic rule we memorized was simple: when you are not sure if it's a good mushroom, don't touch it!

The village of Big Balandino had a club - a spacious wooden building where a large hall was a cultural center. The villagers could dance once a week and watched movies every evening there. Once there was an amateur concert. Our mother persuaded me to read from the stage some poems in Russian and Ukrainian. I was ten-year-old, and apparently, I had some experience of performing. So, the audience received me favorably; perhaps, people were interested to hear Ukrainian, a new language for them.

Almost at the end of our trip, in the village shop, my mother made an unusual purchase: a box of chocolates and a box of cookies. It is possible that this was timed to coincide with the day when grandma Anfissa was born - August, 18. I remember our mother said, "I promised to my mother to do it with my first salary, but during the war I could not. I decided to fulfill my promise now."

I remembered that summer trip well because it was the last time when we met our grandmother Anfissa alive. She died a year and a half later, being eighty years old. Our mother could not come to her funeral: the plane tickets were expensive, and the three-days train journey was too long... I remember that our mother was crying for a few days. Perhaps that was the only situation when we could see her in tears...

I believe that someday we will have another family reunion.

Adventures while driving in England

CAROLYN DONNELL

My one and only trip to England turned into quite the adventure. I had recently reconnected with my birth mother and to celebrate had brought her to England to see where some of our ancestors may have lived.

We stayed at Walton Hall - a manor house turned Bed and Breakfast near Wellesbourne. They operated a van seating no more than 12 guests at a time that traveled to sites like Oxford, Stratford-on-Avon, Warwick castle, and other nearby locations. We received personalized daily tours led by someone who was affiliated with the day's destination. It was wonderful but I also wanted to see sites farther away. I planned on renting a car for one day and driving us to Bath and then to Stonehenge, circling back to home base.

"You really should hire a tour car." The owner of the tour van advised. "Or take the train and join a tour there. I don't advise driving all that way if you have never driven on the left side of a road before."

Hmmph. I've been driving since I was 14. I can handle it. I thought he was probably drumming up business for a cousin.

So I disregarded his words and rented a Honda with my American Express card, complete with full insurance, and set out on the road to Bath. Wasn't long before I realized that the van owner might have had a point. Not only are you on the wrong side of the road. You are also on the wrong side of the car. Throws your perspective off in many ways, especially trying to navigate roundabouts. I got honked at and possibly even cursed at more than once.

Needless to say, I got lost. Every sign I followed that said Bath led me in circles. Perhaps it really was a mysterious place, disappearing like the mists of Avalon in the old legends. I finally saw a sign that said Stonehenge.

What the heck. Stonehenge was next on the list anyway. That destination appeared without much effort. We stopped and checked the gift shop. The site itself was fenced off and could only be viewed from a distance. Someone in the shop said that Avebury was a smaller stone circle nearby where one could have close access to the stones themselves.

Following the map, we cruised around a curve on a narrow blacktop village road. Mom was telling a joke. All of a sudden the rear ends of two horses loomed up in front of us.

"You're gonna hit the horse!" mother screamed.

I jerked the steering wheel to the right. Out of the corner of my eye, I saw rear hooves of one of the horses raise up into the air. They landed with a boom on the side of the left front fender, causing the car to veer from the far left all the way over to the grass on the right. The car came to a stop. Mother and I were still in one piece. Hitting an animal on an English road was supposed to be a big deal. I wondered if I should just get out of the car with my hands outstretched, waiting for the cuffs.

A man with blond curls and a red face came around from behind the horses. Was he the owner? He came to look at the horse's foot.

I could see even from where I stood that the hoof was bleeding. My heart sank.

"Don't you know how to drive?" he yelled.

With tears running down my face, I replied. "No. I have never driven in England before."

He demanded that I follow him to his home nearby where he had his vet come and examine the horse – a registered Arabian mare in foal. A little surge of fear swept through me. I wondered briefly if it was some kind of scam, but knowing something about animal rights in England, I figured I wouldn't have much hope.

He handed me a pen to sign over a traveler's check to pay for the vet visit. The amount was a lot less than I had feared. Fortunately the American Express insurance took care of the cost to the car except for a small deductible.

After I signed, I looked at the writing on the pen. Dodson Feed and Seed. DODSON! Our family name. What a coincidence. Had we come to rest in our ancestor's homeland without even trying?

I tried to get mother's attention, but she was relaxing with a cuppa' the owner's wife had offered her. I wish I had asked more questions, but we were anxious to get back on the road. I didn't keep the pen either. What a souvenir that would have been.

I only got lost twice that evening finding our way back in the dark - English roads don't have lighting - but we finally made it back to Walton Hall in one piece.

I have always wondered if the owner went to the pub that night and said "Hey Dodds, one of your relatives tried to kill my horse today."

Misstep on a Catamaran in Costa Rica

JANET LIPKIN BEIN

While our Costa Rica tour group stayed in Guanacaste, I chose to go on an optional sailing and snorkeling excursion.

As we boarded the catamaran, a crew member said, "Put your backpacks in the cabin and then come to the front deck." I entered the cabin, reached out to put my bag next to other bags on a shelf. And then...

Down, down into blackness. Thumpity, thump. Blinking, I looked about and saw a closed door marked Toilet.

I had fallen down a flight of stairs. During other snorkeling excursions, I had sailed on larger boats with different configurations.

Everyone else had rushed to select prime spots on the deck. Shakily, I pushed to my feet, hobbled up the stairs and onto the deck, where my friend JoAnne had saved a space for me. I told her what happened.

She looked at my puffy left foot. "Oh no! Is the rest of you ok?"

"I think so, other than bruising." I showed her the purple and red blotch adorning my left thigh.

Crew members milled around us about taking orders for unlimited cocktails.

"I need ice packs. I fell down the stairs." I pointed to my swollen left foot, and my left flank. "And a rum coke, please."

I continued quaffing rum cokes, as we sailed along to a tranquil bay, where the boat anchored.

I still wanted to go snorkeling.

"Do you think you can climb back up the steps?" a crew member asked.

Yearning to submerge my aching body in the water, I checked out the feasibility. The boat had two full steps rather than a ladder, and a railing I could grasp. "Yes."

Everyone had to wear a life jacket, which further assured me I would be able to manage in the water. I could not wear fins and couldn't propel myself forward with flutter kicks. But I could use my arms. The water did feel good. Unfortunately, we didn't see any fish.

When I got back up on the boat, our tour guide, Luis wrapped an ace bandage around my foot. "I'll take you to the hotel's clinic as soon as we get back. Do you have travel insurance?"

I nodded.

I texted my husband, Michael. "Don't worry. But I hurt my left ankle and need to get it checked. I left the insurance paperwork on the table near the coffee machine."

Michael was waiting for me with the insurance papers when the van pulled up at the Hotel Tamarindo. Together, Luis, Michael and I made our way to the hotel's clinic.

I showed the receptionist my insurance papers. She handed them back. "We don't have an X-ray machine. You need to go to Hospital Metropolitano."

The recommended destination, Hospital Metropolitano, was located about 40 minutes away by car. A handsome young man name Carlos, who was a manager at the hotel and a friend of Luis, drove us to Hospital Metropolitano. Despite its name it turned out to be not a hospital but merely a private clinic.

They took a couple of X-rays. No fracture. The doctor told me I could continue participating in the tour while wearing a walking boot. I also got a 5-day supply of anti-inflammatory, anti-pain medication.

The accident happened on a Friday, and we were scheduled to hike at Manuel Antonio National Park—a top highlight of the tour—on Sunday. Would I be able to do it?

We spent most of Saturday on a long bus ride from Guanacaste to Manuel Antonio. Fellow travelers commented on the ease with which I seemed to be able to walk with my boot.

My whole foot swelled up during the long bus ride from Guanacaste to Monteverde. But it didn't hurt that much. The bruise on my thigh hurt more than my ankle did. I lay down on the bed with my foot raised and covered the foot with a bag of ice.

"We'll be taking a park trail built to be accessible," Luis told me. "And we go slowly so I can describe what we see. At the end, there's a beach rated as the fifth most beautiful beach in the world."

I love beaches. Michael lent me a hiking pole for additional support. During rough spots from the bus to the trail, I took hold of either Michael or JoAnne. The trail itself was flat and covered with smooth planks. When we reached Playa Manuel Antonio, the beach was every bit as beautiful as I'd anticipated.

I had to remove my boot to go from the picnic table, where we left our gear, into the sea. But it wasn't a large distance and I put as little weight as possible on my foot.

The clear, tranquil, warm water felt therapeutic. We stayed at the beach for two hours and I spent almost the entire time in the water. Too bad that we had to walk another mile and a half to get back to the parking lot. At least, I could wear my boot and use the hiking pole.

The following day we headed back to the capital, San Jose. My ankle swelling and discomfort had increased by that point. I skipped the city walking tour and just joined the group farewell dinner.

The orthopedic boot did give us some advantages at the airports. In Costa Rica, the security guy invited me and Michael to the head of the lines. Back in the USA, I used the airport's wheelchair service and got ushered swiftly through passport control, baggage claim, and delivered to the Uber pickup area.

Happy to get home to California, I got my foot rechecked. They confirmed that there is no fracture. Just swelling, bruising, and pain.

"You overdid things," said my local doctor. "Stay off your feet as much as possible for two to four weeks. And don't do any exercising for four to six weeks."

Despite it all, I'm glad that I was able to complete the trip.

Bad Beds

TERRY A. REPAK

If anything could induce me to stop traveling and stay home, it wouldn't be long security lines, delayed flights, or skyrocketing airfares. It would be the prospect of having to spend another night in another bad hotel bed.

"Bad" is a relative term, of course. For me it means a soft mattress that leaves me with a restless night's sleep and a backache. In four-plus decades of travel, I've found that the pricier the hotel (and Airbnb), the more fluff and frills they put on beds to coddle and impress their guests.

What few hoteliers realize is that many people with the time and money to travel have aging backs; and I, for one, hate frills and fluff on a mattress.

Forget memory foam, which is in vogue in most hotels these days. Such mattresses make your shoulders curve inward and the lower back sink in, encasing you in awkward positions. After a night on a memory foam mattress, I have to do stretching exercises to sooth aching back muscles.

Almost as bad as memory foam are pillow tops, which are also in vogue. Instead of sinking into a mattress, I need the support of a firm yet supple surface across my shoulders and back. A pillow top only works for me when it's positioned on top of a mattress and can be removed, allowing me to re-make the bed without it.

Even at four and five-star hotels, I often end up sleeping on the floor instead of in their deluxe beds. Such was the case in Victoria, Canada, when I booked a hotel overlooking the harbor. At check in, I asked the receptionist if there were any rooms with firm mattresses. She proudly announced that all the mattresses had recently been replaced, but with only one type. The view from my harborside room was riveting, especially at night with the colorful lights reflecting off the water. But when I lay down on the bed, I was engulfed in a plush pillow top that couldn't be removed. Predictably, the next morning I woke up with neck and back pain.

It happens all the time in US hotels too, and in lodges and Airbnb rentals. That's why I always travel with a thin camping mat that can be inflated to a firmness I like. I use it on plush mattresses to make them more rigid across the shoulders and back. If the bed is simply too soft, I'll ask the front desk if they have a twin mattress that goes with a rollaway cot. Such mattresses are usually firm enough if I put them on the floor with my inflatable mat on top.

After living in east and west Africa for a decade, I found that the mattresses in most hotels in major cities are made of dense foam, which works well for me. This is also true in southern Europe and in parts of Mexico. My favorite hotel in a quiet cove north of Puerto Vallarta has quality foam mattresses that are a dream to sleep on.

Is it too much to ask that hotels offer guests a choice of mattresses from firm to plush? I'd love to see an app that rates hotel beds, which travelers could consult before booking a room.

At the risk of sounding like a privileged grump, when paying for a pricey hotel, I'd like to get a good night's sleep that leaves me pain-free in the morning. Forget the memory foam and give me a firm mattress so I don't have to resort to my air mat on the floor.

Not All Those Who Wander Are Lost

WILLIAM JOHN ROSTRON

My wife and I will spend over one hundred days on vacation this year. We will not pack suitcases or wait in lines at airports. No, we have been proud RVers for over forty years (eighteen since retirement). This choice has allowed us to visit the 48 contiguous states, 150 national parks, all 30 major league baseball stadiums, two Canadian Provinces, and scores of quite unusual places.

Many people would eschew our method of travel, opting for first-class hotels with all the latest amenities. But we aren't suffering. Our children are fond of telling us it isn't camping when you have four flat-screen TVs, central air conditioning, a residential-size refrigerator, and a washer and dryer. Our unique way of travel is not roughing it, and since retirement, we have journeyed on 45 major trips totaling 150,000 miles.

Sometimes, we wander with no particular destination or timetable. It gives us a freedom seldom felt in a modern world where everything follows a schedule. The phrase "Not All Those Who Wander..." is lifted from the J.R.R. Tolkien book The Hobbit, but it couldn't describe our lifestyle any better if we had created it ourselves. Though we have seen all the traditional tourist attractions (Yellowstone is our favorite), we often roam out of our way locations to seek the weird and unusual. We love discovering places, attractions, and events off the beaten path.

Last winter, we took a "Polar Plunge." These rapidly growing phenomena have participants jumping into the ocean in February. Usually, these are done as fundraisers for worthy causes; the one we participated in was no exception. We got our requisite "Polar Plunge 2023" tee shirt and readied to enter the churning seas. Did I forget to mention that we did this in Key West, and the water temps were in the 80s? Yes, this tongue-in-cheek party was great fun and raised bundles of money.

Did you ever go sledding without snow? The White Sands of Alamogordo, New Mexico, are actually a super fine form of gypsum conducive to sledding down them. This activity is even encouraged by National Park officials... with one caveat. White Sands is also a missile testing ground for the United States. Potential sledders must call in advance to ensure no tests are scheduled on the day they wish to come. A communication breakdown could prove quite exciting.

Our California excursion included all the staple tourist attractions of Yosemite: giant redwoods, the Golden Gate Bridge, the Pacific Coast Highway, Hollywood, and so much more. But how many people visit the site of the tragedy of the Donner Pass? It seemed the height of irony when we left the location where trapped 19th-century pioneers resorted to cannibalism and soon were in an all-you-can-eat buffet in Reno.

In Minnesota, we visited the controversial Kensington Runestone, a stone with ancient markings that claim its Viking writers were under attack and about to be wiped out by local natives. This event supposedly happened centuries before Columbus and other explorers "found" the New World. I don't know if it was real, but the locals have based their entire economy on its veracity.

For my part, it gave new meaning to the Minnesota Viking football team.

On the coast of Oregon, we visited the small town of Astoria, which presents many unique experiences. It is where Lewis and Clark arrived at the Pacific Ocean. Harbor seals by the score frolic in the bay across from tours of the house where the classic movie "Goonies" was filmed. Juxtaposed with this lively town, a few hours away is Mt. St. Helens and its tale of horror. The long ride up to view the crater includes views of the destruction this volcanic eruption wrought, giving visible proof of nature's power.

These are just a handful of the hundreds of incredible experiences we have enjoyed. I could go on and on about the mysterious Cahokia Mounds in Illinois or sitting in Wild Bill Hickok's "death" seat in Deadwood. Perhaps I could tell you about how two Buffalo fought each other with our jeep in the middle in Yellowstone or how we climbed an outside adder of a cliff dwelling a thousand feet high in Mesa Verde. You may be interested in the underground city beneath Seattle or Roswell, New Mexico, a city whose streetlights are glass facsimiles of aliens. If food is your thing, I could go about Cincinnati's version of Chili, Native American flatbread, North Dakota's Pitchfork Barbeque, and Rocky Mountain oysters (which, as many know, are not shellfish).

Lest I give the impression that it all was wonderful, I could mention the locust swarm in Kansas and the four times we had to evacuate an area because of coming hurricanes on the East Coast. And there is so much more.

After four decades, I realized that traveling might get harder at some point. Therefore, we have also adopted a second slogan that I found on a tee shirt in a Smokey Mountain gift shop.

You don't stop having adventures because you get old...You get old because you stopped having adventures.

Crossing America by Train

JASMINE TRITTEN

While sitting on the train, traveling across America from New York to San Francisco, I suddenly panicked about our next stop in Chicago. My Danish girlfriend and I faced a seven-hour layover at Union Station. Everybody in Denmark warned us, before we left our country, about gangsters in Chicago. What to do?

Exhausted and vulnerable, we arrived at the train station's main hall, carrying all our baggage. They also told us in Denmark not to trust anybody. Large blisters from the heavy luggage oozed into our palms. Finally, we found a bench and flopped down, surrounded by our suitcases. Soon men of all ages, sizes, and shapes flocked around us, simultaneously charming and harassing us.

Obviously, we attracted them like magnets with our beautifully innocent Scandinavian looks and naive appearances. How easy it would be for somebody to steal a piece of luggage from us. How can we possibly relax like this? Fending off strangers tired us out. The smell in the station hit my nostrils and annoyed me. Besides, the noise of the place became unbearable.

"Let's go to the ladies' room to rest," I suggested to my girlfriend. We dragged our luggage inside the women's powder room and crashed into some dirty, pink lounge chairs. Safely in a corner, we hoped nobody would disturb us. At last, we might be able to get some peace until our train left for the wild west. I closed my eyes. Imagine spending almost seven hours in the ladies' room of Union Station in Chicago. I cannot believe it.

After hiding out for seven hours, we boarded the train heading for California. Inside the compartment across from us sat two little boys. They traveled alone. We adopted them right away. A large cage containing five chicken hawk babies filled the seat next to them. Soon the boys opened the confined space and let out the little creatures.

Immediately, the small birds jumped on top of our shoulders, knees, and hands, making droppings all over, but we did not mind. Rather we enjoyed the unusual experience and took turns with the boys to get raw meat from the train's kitchen to feed them. I wonder why the boys travel alone. But we had too much fun with the hawk babies to think about anything else.

When not attending to the birds, we leaped into the observation car. We watched the landscape change through large windows from flat green farmland to rolling hills, mountains, and deserts as our train approached the Western states of America. Each time we came to a crossing, the sounds of bells and whistles filled our ears, and lights flashed as the arm came down across the roads.

I scanned the landscape for cowboys as we passed by with the train for days but did not spot any. Where are they? Since arriving in the United States, I dreamed of seeing a real cowboy. As a little girl growing up in Denmark, I used to watch cowboy movies and shows where they were heroes, and cowboys have intrigued and fascinated me ever since.

At long last, I spotted a cowboy on a horse, working cattle in a large field. I jumped up and down, yelling, "A cowboy! A cowboy! A real cowboy! Hurrah!" My girlfriend hurried over to join me. Ecstatic and loud, we startled everybody around us. People stared at us, but we did not care. This was a big moment for us, witnessing a real live cowboy on a horse rather than the actors we had watched on movie screens in Denmark.

My dream had materialized. Little did I know at the time cowboys were ordinary people who spit and swore. Some even chewed tobacco. We approached Fresno in California, where we planned to spend time with some friends of our parents. The family received us with open arms. One day, the daughter in the family hinted, as she drove us in her black convertible sports car with the top down, "We are going to visit the most beautiful little village in America."

The moment we drove down Ocean Avenue through the village of Carmel-by-the-Sea, I felt at home and peaceful in my soul. Warmth spread through every cell of my body. The tall pine trees, the small Hans & Gretchen houses, the vast ocean, and the surrounding hills literally swallowed me up. For three days, we stayed at the charming Stone House Inn. For the first time in my life, I was in Heaven. Intoxicated.

Every day, we walked around the village, visiting one art gallery after another, talking with the artists about their paintings and sculptures. A Mecca for art. When the smell and breeze of the Pacific Ocean reached my nostrils and the sounds of the sea lions hit my ears, I became hypnotized.

"This is where I want to live," I suddenly blasted to my girlfriend. "This is it. I want to start from scratch in this charming place rather than live in a big city. We can always move to San Francisco later."

"You know, I feel the same way about it! Let's stay here instead," she answered. What a relief. She feels the same way I do about changing our plans.

So, our original goal miraculously changed into staying in Carmel without seeing the much-talked-about Golden Gate Bridge in San Francisco. My gut said yes. We found a small white house on top of the hill in Carmel with two bedrooms and a fireplace for a reasonable monthly rent. How amazing. Meant to be. Within a short time, we landed jobs.

The train took us almost all the way from the East Coast to the West Coast. Happily, we began our new lives in this charming little village on the other side of the earth from Denmark. Everything felt so right, as if we were guided from above to our new home in America.

Unexpected Gift

JANET METZ WALTER

Twas the night before Christmas Eve. The airport was teeming with humanity, planning to get out in time to spend Christmas Eve with family or friends, or on a happy vacation.

We were on our way to Nassau Bahamas where we would spend a few days before heading off to visit Grandma and Grandpa in Florida.

The luggage was aboard the plane, we were all seated waiting to take off when there was an announcement: "The plane is overbooked and there is too much luggage on the plane. The plane is too heavy to take off. We need at least six people to get off the plane."

Everyone looked around. What does that mean? Who are they kicking off?

Then came the next announcement: "We will credit anyone who volunteers to get off the plane one hundred and fifty dollars."

What? That isn't even enough to pay for the ticket. No one

moved. It became an auction: "Two hundred dollars." Heads shook "No." "Five hundred dollars." The kids looked at us.

"We have hotel reservations," my husband said. "We are not getting off."

In desperation the crew kept consulting with their superiors. At $750 one person got off.

At $1000 two more people. We saw people consulting with each other, arguing with each other and other people starting to get upset that we were not leaving.

"Fifteen hundred dollars." My husband jumped up. "OK we have four here!" That shocked the crew and the passengers but now they had their six people and even one extra.

"I thought we had hotel reservations!" my son exclaimed.

"Fifteen hundred dollars a piece gives us $6000," my husband explained.

"That's a lot of money for traveling. We'll call the hotel and change the reservations."

We were well aware that it did not go exactly as expected for the airline. We got off the plane listening to murmurs of frustration, and happiness that now the plane would finally be taking off, after they found all the luggage of course.

"Don't worry," the flight attendant said. "There is another plane taking off at the next gate and you will probably be able to get on it."

Even the kids said "Who are they kidding? This place is packed. Every plane is probably just like this one unless there is one going to Alaska or someplace;" But we dutifully shlepped our luggage and carryon's over to the next gate only to be told as expected,

"Why did they send you here? Are they nuts? You are probably not getting out tonight."

The agent pointed to a desk. "Speak to the people over there. They will help you find hotel reservations and will get you on a plane in the morning."

We didn't have high hopes. We figured our vacation was a bust and we would just have to go straight to Florida whenever we could get a flight.

Surprisingly we were wrong. There was a flight the next morning that had seats because it was Christmas Eve day and a lot of people had left today. They got us a hotel room at the airport. They handed us our $6000 in airline vouchers, but we were not leaving it at that.

"What happens if the hotel in Nassau doesn't refund our money?' My husband asked. "And don't we have to eat breakfast in the morning?"

The clerk at the desk made a phone call.

"OK" he announced. "We will give you an extra thousand a piece."

We almost fell over but tried to remain calm. We were figuring about a few hundred total.

We got the voucher.. Someone had made a mistake. The voucher was for $5000. Now we had a total of $11,000.

We probably held the record for the most money for one family in vouchers.

The airlines must have changed their policy after that because we never saw or heard of anyone getting that much money again.

We couldn't use the vouchers right away because we already had a trip to Japan booked for the summer but we had a lot of nice trips in the following few years.

Stay tuned!

How TSA Can Save Your Life

MATT J. MCGEE

Spencer Northman was as surprised as anyone else the day the TSA told him he wasn't going to be allowed to fly to Buffalo.

He'd taken off his shoes. He'd separated his laptop from his carry-on. He'd raised his arms for the full-body scan.

Then a foreman waved him aside. Minutes later, an intense looking middle-aged man appeared in a bland gray suit a government salary allows.

SONNY his nametag read. Spencer immediately thought of Al Pacino's accomplice in Dog Day Afternoon.

"I'm sorry to be the bearer of bad news Mr. Northman, but apparently we won't be able to let you on the plane today," Sonny said.

Spencer usually avoided arguments. Today, though, felt different. "I've been flying," he said, "since I was twelve. I haven't so much as snored on a flight."

"I understand."

"So what's wrong?"

Sonny lowered his head and, seemingly against his better judgment, motioned Spencer to follow. Spencer followed to a nearby office. Sonny sat behind a desk. He motioned for Spencer to take the interview chair.

"Is this your first time through the full-body scan, Mr. Northman?"

"This year, yes. What's that..." Spencer's expression quickly became concern. "What is it? Is it," he whispered, "is it cancer?"

"No no," Sonny smiled. "Machines aren't that good yet. This isn't any of my business Mr. Northman but..."

"Spit it out."

"Have you had any kind of surgery recently?"

Spencer's eyes squinted slowly. "Gallbladder. Two months ago. It's the only operation I've ever had. How did ...?"

Sonny reached across his desk, an all-steel, military issue hand-me-down his station would receive. He opened a file and pushed a gray printout into Spencer's view.

It looked like an ultrasound. Spencer saw a liver, a heart. Somewhere near the shadow of his left lung was a shiny white curlicue.

"What is that?"

"That," Sonny said, "appears to be a surgical clamp. Can't be sure of course. But the department has seen things like this before."

Spenser's mouth dropped like a guppy. Words eventually came. "You're kidding. Some hack... I paid twenty grand ... out of my own pocket and they left a clamp in me??"

Sonny held out his hands in a 'slow down' motion. "I understand you're upset. I won't blame you if you're going to want to sue someone.."

"Sue?? Are you kidding me? I'm going to find a doctor who'll take this thing outta me, then I'm gonna find the guy who left it in there and have it surgically implanted through his nose. Sue? He'll wish I just sued him."

"I can't have you talking about committing acts of violence in my presence, otherwise - "

"Otherwise what? I already can't fly. What could I lose?"

"Future privileges," Sonny shrugged.

Spencer shook his head. "Is this why I've had trouble losing weight?"

"I'm not a doctor."

Spencer released a long, hard exhale. "This isn't your fault. Look. I need to get to Buffalo. My family's expecting me. What can we do."

Sonny remembered how, when his son turned three, he'd asked an incessant string of questions. What makes clouds? Why do people wear glasses? How do trees grow?

Sonny, much to his own surprise, had an answer for everything. Clouds are made by birds farting in the sky – if you ever see a big flock of birds you know it's gonna be a cloudy day. People wear glasses to keep their noses from falling off. Trees grow so they don't stay small and get mistaken for shrubs. No one respects a shrub but everyone looks up to a tree.

Sonny smiled at Spencer and folded hands. "I've got an idea."

There is a make-shift clinic in every airport, smaller than a walk-in closet and eternally ready as a triage unit. Sonny left Spencer in capable hands and returned to his post.

"So," said the doctor, "what seems to be wrong today?"

Spencer handed over the full body scan. The doctor spun it around and crunched his brow.

"Wow, someone left a clamp in you."

"It seems to be holding me up from getting to Buffalo. Got any ideas?"

"Besides taking a train?"

Spencer didn't laugh.

"Sorry. Yes, I think I can pencil this thing through."

Spencer reentered the TSA checkpoint, his flight still half an hour away. This is exactly why I arrive early, he thought, in case someone leaves a medical instrument inside me.

Sonny clicked one of the ropes. Spencer hiked his bag up his shoulder and approached.

"Back again?"

"Doctor says I'm cured."

Spencer handed Sonny the black and white printout. The clamp had been shaded with a number two pencil. At the top right, in red marker a doctor's notation: PATIENT CURED punctuated with a smiley face.

Sonny nodded. "All fixed up?"

"Yep. Wanna see my scar?"

Spencer exposed a gym-toned, lightly hairy chest. In the middle was a fresh Band-Aid. "Now," Spencer said, "to those cameras, you've done your due diligence. May I go see my family in Buffalo?"

Sonny opened a desk drawer and found a stamp that said APPROVED. He then took out 'CONFIDENTIAL,' RUSH DELIVERY' and 'OK.' He handed Spencer the printout with his boarding pass and ticket.

"Safe travels."

As the plane taxied on the runway, Spencer scrolled his cell's contacts. He knew the medical malpractice attorney who'd gone after the manufacturer of the seatbelt that had failed and killed Dale Earnhardt.

Spencer shot him a text then shut off his phone.

Spencer felt the band-aid thru his shirt. It pulled at the hair on his chest. The plane ascended and he settled in, aimed for a city whose football team comes close but never wins championships. He'd often admired Buffalo and its people for their tendency toward common sense. Now, after this episode in L.A., he realized that kind of thing can happen anywhere if you just have a sense of humor about it.

South-Bound on the Oaxaqueño

LORRAINE CAPUTO

13-14 November 1988
El Oaxaqueño (Mexico City to Oaxaca), 1ª numerada

NIGHT

I arrived at the train station with ten minutes to spare, running around to find the Oaxaqueño's platform, nervous with the anticipation, with the worry of missing my first train ride. Gene, Raúl & Rosario, their children Miguel & Joana, fared me well at the gates. Their son kissed me on the cheek.

I settle in. Three men in brown leather jackets walk through. We are told to pull our shades because of rocks. Not resisting temptation, I peek under the corner of mine & see the eerily lit shantytowns.

I pass the time sketching the old man across from me. Upon this page I capture his high forehead, high cheekbones, long Roman nose, his thinned hair. He reads a small book with a magnifying glass.

~

At the blue-tiled San Lorenzo station, a young man with headphones on sits in the office. In front of him are four old-fashioned telegraph machines. The leather-coated men walk back & forth along the train. One has a crowbar. Another holds a walkie-talkie. He walks into the station office.

Off in the distance is a string of city lights. Beyond them are mountains. The altitude aches my head.

~ ~

Just about everyone else has fallen asleep. I look out the window. The edge of the mountain is near this train. Pine trees silhouette against the night. I hear the strained chug of the engine up ahead.

~ ~ ~

By the middle of the night it has become unbelievably cold. I wrap my wool blanket about me. All the other passengers are asleep, bundled in this unheated car. The train personnel walk through, wearing parkas.

MORNING

In the coming light of morning, more becomes visible. The mountains are heavily forested with green curtains occasionally worn thread-bare brown. Below falls a meandering river. Branches scratch the side of this train.

~

We pass by a cemetery nestled in the woods.

A campesino stands behind a large gate, his arms behind him.

Orchards of papaya trees, a few palms ... & banana saplings.

We cross over an orange trestle bridge.

Through a town where people watch this train go by. Others go on with their daily lives.

~ ~

The river thins & boils with rapids as we near its source. The mountains reveal their faulting & tilting.

Forests of saguaro cactus cut their own tree line across the heights.

~ ~ ~

The train winds & winds through this range. The sun is beginning to clear its peaks.

& after a while that sunlight brightens this valley. A couple walking along the sandbars waves at our train.

~ ~ ~ ~

A boy leads a burro, boxes hanging on either side. An old man walks behind.

A teacher stands at the schoolhouse door. The children look out the windows.

~ ~ ~ ~ ~

As we reach the heights of this montaña, I see the top of the valley below & rows upon rows of mountains unfolding beyond.

We click through rock passes.

& frequently stop at towns for a few moments. The ratchet of a jack echoes from between the cars.

~ ~ ~ ~ ~ ~

We clack through rock passes shielding us from the mid-morn sun. Through the spaces of this stone landscape, valleys spread between mountains. & we are descending, descending towards our final station.

Percorso

JOSEPH A. FARINA

I
roman domes and fountains quicken my blood
masterpieces of travertine marble and engineered water
leave me breathless in its magic and fluid eternity.

night
amplifies the feral sounds
among the alleyways and ruins.
cats stalk ,
announcing their kills
with hard growls of pleasure-
they are the true romans here
they come and go at will
among the eternal stones
under their goddess's moon.
they fornicate capriciously
marking the sacred way
for Aradia * with their revelry

splendor, blood and cruel death
fill the coliseum's empty places
the throng that fills its scarred
walkways buzz like drunken flies
a babble of voices rising above
this cauldron of ancient slaughter
redeemed by the wooden cross
anchored to its pitted stones
photographed, a souvenir
of torture, penitent by history
and tourists

II
the tuscan horizon
boasts olive trees and vineyards
manicured in perfect rows
just like the postcards that seduced
us to travel here but without
the thumbtacks holding up
this evenings terra cotta sky.
chiaro scurro furrows and olive orchards
embrace the hill sides
in precise patterns.
Lime white gravel roads
bordered by Mediterranean cypress
cut through the pastoral tapestry
to unseen villas and villages

stone towers stand silently
in the distant, remnants of
medieval fortresses.
I breath deep the intoxicating belvedere (panorama)
sear its depth and colours into my soul
make love to it in silent song
and poetry, root my feet into its soil

becoming
through it, with it, and in it
under the golden tuscan light

IV

Venice
jewel, queen, angel, whore
of the Adriatic.
gondolas, black lacquered
edged in gold, covered against the rain
tethered to striped palinas (poles)
prance in the uneasy surf
with rain and acqua alta (high water)
venice transforms
into a city of umbrellas
clogging tight lanes
pressing in on narrow bridges
the gray light forming a
spectrum of colourful canopies
deflecting the October rain
San Marco-empty-flooding
its perimeter of raised walkways
circled by a babylon of voices and
bright umbrellas

leaves flutter and fall in the ocean wind
salt spray anoints
the paved stones of San Marco's square
tears at our departure

* (Roman cat goddess)

Hinerary Planning

Questions to Plan the
Perfect Getaway

Narrowing Down the Choices

Whether you are planning a solo jaunt or a group adventure, the following are some of the questions you will want to address with all travelers (or at least the ones who are footing the bill!).

Have you decided exactly where you wish to go? (List destination and/or possibilities)

_____
_____
_____
_____
_____
_____

Have you decided exactly when you wish to go? (Season/exact dates/holiday/etc.)

_____
_____
_____
_____
_____
_____

Or if you are exploring options, think about the following:

I would like the weather to be:

(warmer? colder? doesn't matter?)

_____
_____
_____

_____

I would like to: stay in one place? Travel to various sites?

_____
_____
_____
_____
_____

I am most interested in (write words such as those below):

relaxation - cultural experiences - fine dining - adventure

_____
_____
_____
_____
_____
_____

I wish to travel by:

Car - train - plane - boat - other

_____
_____

_____
_____
_____

I want to come home with:

_____
_____
_____
_____
_____
_____

Something I definitely do NOT want to do/see is:

_____
_____
_____
_____
_____

Do I wish to combine leisure travel with business or family visits? If so, how?

_____
_____

_____

_____

_____

_____

Previously I had a problem with ____ while traveling, so let's avoid:

_____

_____

_____

_____

_____

If you have a number of people you are trying to please with a destination, once you have narrowed down a list you could have each person secretly rank the possibilities in order of preference. Tally the votes, and the destination with the lowest number—thus, more people's preference—is the winner.

Transportation Worksheet

Transportation is an integral part of any trip—whether it is getting to and from your destination, or transportation around once you get there. Sometimes you may have options in your mode of transportation—and even in the comfort level of your transport—while other times you may be resigned to whatever is available. In either case, give some thought to your preferences—yours as well as your travel companions.

If you have already selected your ultimate destination, what is your preferred method of transportation to get there? Is it plane? Train? Car? Bus? Boat? Why is that the preferred method?

_____
_____
_____
_____
_____
_____

If your preferred primary method has different levels of comfort, which is your preference? Comfort level may be a balance between preferences and budget, so consider that when selecting.

_____
_____
_____
_____
_____
_____

If you selected a premium comfort level in the previous question and need to balance your travel budget, where are you willing to compromise?

_____
_____

_____

_____

Do you prefer to make your own transportation arrangements? If not, who will make your travel arrangements for you?

_____

_____

_____

_____

What are the exact dates that you will be traveling to and from your ultimate destination?

Depart for your trip:

_____

_____

Return home:

_____

_____

Additional important travel dates:

_____

_____

Do you prefer to travel by day? Overnight?

_____

_____

_____

Do you have preferred airlines or other companies for your travels?

_____

_____

_____

Please list any frequent flyer numbers or other travel access numbers below:

_____

_____

_____

_____

_____

While at your destination, will you be in need of transportation?

Consider first any transportation needs from your primary transportation to your accommodations (such as, from the airport to your hotel). Will you be needing a shuttle bus? Taxi/Uber? Monorail? Something else?

How about additional transportation at your destination—will you be renting a car? Relying on public transportation (trains/buses)? Taking taxis/Ubers?

Have you had a poor experience with transportation that you would like to avoid in the future? Was it due to a weather event? Poor service from a company? Something else? Briefly describe the incident below.

_____

_____

Due to this incident, will you be avoiding a particular season/holiday? Company? Something else?

_____

_____

_____

_____

_____

_____

Lodging Worksheet

Where you stay on your trip can range from the most important aspect—such as with an all-inclusive resort—or simply a place to lay your head while tackling your itinerary. When my daughter was traveling around Europe, she would purposely sleep on overnight trains or buses so that she would wake up in a new city without skipping a beat. While most wouldn't consider such lodging relaxing, it illustrates that there is a range of what travelers are seeking in lodging.

In order to narrow your choices, consider the following statements and rank from 1 to 5 whether you agree or disagree with each.

1 = strongly agree
2 = somewhat agree
3 = this doesn't matter ,much to me
4 = somewhat disagree
5 = strongly disagree

Staying in luxury accommodations is very important to me.

    1   2   3   4   5

I would like to have a stellar view from my room.

    1   2   3   4   5

A full kitchen would help us to save money on meals.

    1   2   3   4   5

I will not be spending much time at our accommodations, as we will be busy elsewhere with sightseeing/activities.

    1   2   3   4   5

I would like the place we stay to have activities and amenities on-site.

    1   2   3   4   5

It would be preferable to be within walking distance of a town/city.

    1   2   3   4   5

I need laundry facilities to clean clothes during my stay.

    1   2   3   4   5

The location should include a spacious living area for lounging or socializing.

        1   2   3   4   5

I prefer a quiet and secluded setting to a lively atmosphere.

        1   2   3   4   5

I am traveling with pets, and I need pet-friendly accommodations.

        1   2   3   4   5

I need multiple bedrooms or suites for privacy or family use.

        1   2   3   4   5

My group requires accessible accommodations for mobility or other needs.

        1   2   3   4   5

I especially enjoy staying in a unique property, such as a historic inn or eco-lodge.

        1   2   3   4   5

My preference is for an all-inclusive package that covers meals, drinks, and activities?

        1   2   3   4   5

Think about your favorite place where you have stayed. What features made that stay especially memorable?

_____

_____

_____

_____

_____

_____

How about the worst place where you have stayed. What happened that you would like to avoid in the future?

_____

_____

_____

_____

_____

_____

List below any preferred companies, along with loyalty numbers/programs for easy reference. Also, if you have special rates or incentives with particular vendors, include them below:

_____

_____

_____

_____

_____

_____

_____

What are the exact dates that you will require accommodation?

Arrival:

_____

Departure:
_____

_____

If you will be needing more than one accommodation, list the dates for each below:

_____

_____

_____

_____

_____

_____

Restaurants and Experiences

While some love fine dining, seeing shows and visiting museums, others are all about packing a backpack, visiting theme parks, or hiking in national parks. With my own family, I have always given them a questionnaire to learn more about each person's desires for a trip, and tried to include at least some from each "wish list." To get the ball rolling, consider the following:

Food/Dining

Do you prefer fine dining, casual eateries, or street food experiences while traveling?

___

Are you interested in trying the local cuisine, or do you prefer familiar food options?

___

Do you like to visit local farmers' markets or food festivals on vacation?

___

Would you be interested in a cooking class to learn local recipes?

___

Do you want to visit Michelin-starred restaurants or high-end eateries?

___

Are you open to adventurous food experiences, like trying unusual or exotic dishes?

___

Do you enjoy food tours or wine and spirits tastings as part of your vacation?

___

Will you need vegetarian, vegan, gluten-free, or other specific dining options?

___

Do you prefer dining in scenic locations like beachside cafes or rooftop restaurants?

Are you interested in going to food trucks or casual pop-up restaurants for a more local vibe?

Would you prefer to explore street food markets over formal restaurants?

Are there any food-related attractions you'd like to visit, like chocolate factories or breweries?

Activities/Attractions

Do you enjoy visiting theme parks or would you rather explore cultural landmarks?

Are you excited about spending a day hiking, or would you prefer a city walking tour?

How interested are you in seeing live shows, performances, or theater productions?

Would you like to visit museums, art galleries, or historical sites on this trip?

Are there any sports or outdoor activities you want to try, like surfing or skiing?

Do you enjoy water-based activities, such as snorkeling, kayaking, or boat tours?

Would you like to visit national parks and nature reserves, or do you prefer urban exploration?

Do you enjoy shopping and browsing local markets or boutiques as part of your trip?

Are amusement parks or theme parks a must for your vacation experience?

Would you prefer to spend your days relaxing at the beach, spa, or pool, or exploring new sights?

Are there any festivals, parades, or local events you'd like to experience while on vacation?

One of the joys of solo travel is that you get to do exactly as you please, and the answers to this questionnaire can form the backbone of your itinerary. If traveling with others, compromise may be key, but including at least one "must do" from each person's preferred activities will make for a more enjoyable group trip for all.

Packing and Luggage

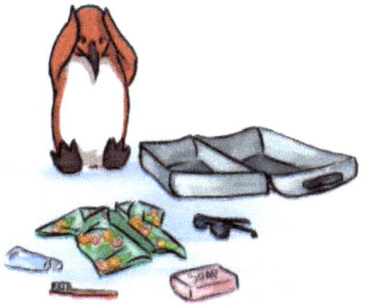

Most travelers overpack. Honestly—I have stood watching with wonder the majority of people struggling with large suitcases as they leave the airport ... in Hawaii, where very little clothing is needed. And I'm not talking only about parents with baby gear or older adults who may be carrying a CPAP machine—I'm talking about 20 somethings on a fun vacation.

Now that most airlines charge for extra luggage, overpacking isn't just an inconvenience, it is an unnecessary expense. Couple that with the fact that more than two million bags are lost by the airlines each year, and perhaps you'll agree that packing lighter is a great way to save money—and stress—on vacation.

The biggest detriment to packing light is indecision. Most travelers think that having more gives them more options when away, but in actuality, they return home with plenty of unused items. If one could decide in advance—keeping in mind the typical climate and planned activities for each day—what is needed and select clothing for each day rather than carry an entire wardrobe, your luggage would be infinitely lighter. To that end, creating a packing list is key, so that all needs are addressed in advance, and nothing extraneous is dragged along.

Here's a detailed, universal packing list broken down into categories that can be tailored to any destination, climate, or person:

Clothing

Essentials

- Underwear (enough for each day of the trip + extras)
- Socks (appropriate for the climate)
- Pajamas / sleepwear
- T-shirts / tops (casual and dressy options)
- Pants / jeans / skirts
- Shorts (for warm climates)
- Sweaters / hoodies
- Jacket / coat (light, medium, or heavy depending on climate)
- Shoes (comfortable walking shoes, dress shoes, sandals, or boots)
- Belts / suspenders

Climate-Specific

- Swimsuits / cover-ups (beach or pool)
- Flip-flops or water shoes (beach or pool)
- Rain jacket or umbrella (rainy destinations)
- Thermal layers (cold climates)
- Hat, gloves, scarf (for cold weather)
- Sun hat / cap (for hot weather)
- Sunglasses

Toiletries

Basic Toiletries

- Toothbrush and toothpaste
- Shampoo and conditioner (travel-size or full-size)
- Soap or body wash
- Deodorant
- Razor and shaving cream
- Hairbrush or comb
- Hair ties, clips, or accessories
- Travel-size perfume or cologne

Skin & Body Care

- Sunscreen (face and body)
- Lip balm with SPF
- Moisturizer (face and body)
- After-sun lotion or aloe vera (if going to sunny destinations)
- Hand sanitizer
- Face wipes or makeup remover
- Insect repellent (if needed)

For Women

- Makeup essentials (foundation, mascara, lip gloss, etc.)
- Menstrual products (pads, tampons, menstrual cup, etc.)
- Hair styling tools (hairdryer, straightener, curling iron)

For Men

- Beard grooming kit (if needed)
- Aftershave
- Hair gel or styling cream

Electronics

- Phone and charger
- Laptop / tablet and charger
- Portable power bank
- Headphones or earbuds
- Travel adapters (if going abroad)
- Camera and extra memory cards / batteries
- E-reader (if desired)
- Bluetooth speaker (optional)

Travel Documents & Essentials

- Passport and/or driver's license
- Boarding passes and travel itinerary
- Copies of important documents (passport, insurance, ID)
- Travel insurance documents
- Credit cards, cash (local currency), and travel wallet
- Health insurance card
- Emergency contact information
- Vaccination card / health information (if required)

- Pen and notebook
- Guidebooks or maps

Health & Medications

- Prescription medications (in labeled containers)
- Pain relievers (ibuprofen, aspirin, etc.)
- First aid kit (band-aids, antiseptic wipes, etc.)
- Motion sickness remedies
- Allergy medication
- Vitamins / supplements
- Cold or flu medication (in case you get sick)
- Hand sanitizer and disinfecting wipes
- Contact lenses and solution (if applicable)
- Glasses (regular or reading)

Accessories

- Jewelry (consider leaving valuables at home)
- Watch
- Lightweight backpack or day bag
- Tote bag / reusable shopping bag
- Scarf or shawl (multi-purpose)
- Travel pillow, blanket, and eye mask (for flights)
- Earplugs and/or noise-canceling headphones
- Refillable water bottle
- Snacks for travel
- Ziplock bags or packing cubes for organization

Leisure & Activities

- Books, magazines, or puzzles for entertainment
- Travel journal and pen
- Swimsuit cover-up (beach or pool)
- Travel-sized games or playing cards

- Lightweight sports equipment (yoga mat, frisbee, etc.)
- Travel-sized sewing kit (for emergencies)
- Beach towel or quick-dry towel
- Binoculars (for sightseeing or wildlife viewing)

Miscellaneous

- Laundry bag or plastic bag for dirty clothes
- Travel-sized laundry detergent (for hand-washing clothes)
- Luggage tags
- Locks for luggage
- Extra batteries for electronics
- Reusable utensils or travel cutlery (for meals on the go)
- Emergency sewing kit or safety pins

This comprehensive list should cover just about any type of trip, allowing travelers to adjust based on destination, activities, and personal preferences!

Recap and Lessons Learned

What to include and avoid the next time you travel

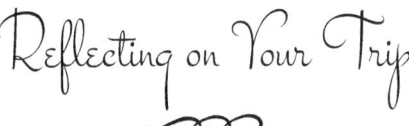

Reflecting on Your Trip

Ahhh ... memories! Perhaps on your way home—or soon afterwards before your memories begin to fade—consider the following questions to reminisce and learn from your recent trip.

The best food I had was:

_____
_____
_____
_____
_____
_____

The worst weather was:

_____
_____
_____
_____
_____
_____

The most memorable person I met was:

_____
_____
_____
_____
_____
_____

The most unique thing I saw/did was:

_____
_____
_____
_____
_____
_____

Let's hope THIS never happens again:

_____
_____
_____
_____
_____
_____

I'd really like to go back to:

_____
_____
_____
_____
_____
_____

The lesson I learned was:

_____
_____
_____
_____
_____
_____

Eating and Drinking

All that eating out on a journey could either make or break your trip, depending upon whether the food was delicious or caused dysentery! Reflecting on your trip:

TRAVEL TALES & TIPS

What was the best meal you had?

_____
_____
_____
_____
_____
_____

What was the worst meal you had?

_____
_____
_____
_____
_____
_____

What was something you ate for the first time?

_____
_____
_____
_____
_____
_____

What are you hoping to never eat again?

_____
_____
_____
_____
_____
_____

What was the most expensive meal of the trip? (and was it worth it?)

_____
_____
_____
_____
_____
_____

Which meal would you like to cook yourself?

_____
_____
_____
_____
_____
_____

Presentation is often the best part — what was the nicest looking food/meal you had?

_____
_____
_____
_____
_____
_____

Transportation

For some, the journey is half the fun, but for others, transportation issues nearly ruined the adventure. It's all in the details — what was something that made you smile, whether it was a great movie on board, a nice seatmate, or surprisingly little traffic? Reflecting on your trip:

What was your favorite mode of transport? Why?

___

What was something you rode/did for the first time?

___

What are you hoping to never happen again when traveling?

___

What was the most flight/taxi/leg of the trip? (and was it worth it?)

___

What would you do differently next time?

___

Activities

For some, a trip filled with sights and sounds, hustling from one activity to another is bliss, while for others, endless empty days is ideal. Whether you were on the go or on the beach, think back to what was most memorable—both the good, the bad, and the ugly.

What activity did you most enjoyed?

_____

_____

Would all of your traveling companions agree on your choice? If not, what were some highlights for others that you perhaps could have done without?

_____

_____

_____

What was the worst event/excursion of your trip? Did something go wrong, or did everything go as expected, yet you simply didn't enjoy it at all?

_____

_____

_____

_____

_____

What was something you did for the first time?

_____

_____

_____

_____

_____

_____

What are you hoping to never do again?

_____

_____

_____

_____

_____

_____

What was the most expensive activity of your trip? (and was it worth it?)

_____

_____

_____

_____

_____

_____

What did you wish you had done at this particular location but missed out on?

_____

_____
_____
_____
_____
_____

Sometimes an event is exactly what we expected it to be (for better or for worse!) while other times it is much better than expected or much worse than expected. For each of these possibilities, think about an activity from your trip that fits the bill and describe it.

What was better than you expected it to be?

_____
_____
_____
_____

What was worse than you expected it to be?

_____
_____
_____
_____

What was exactly like you expected it to be?

_____
_____
_____

TRAVEL TALES & TIPS

Daily Trip Journal

Remembering the food, friends, and fun after your vacation

Daily Travel Journal

Today's Date _____

The weather was _____

I woke up ... (where? When? Anything notable?) _____
_____

I went to bed ... (where? When? Anything notable?) _____
_____

Today's transportation included: walking car bus train plane bike boat
other: _____
_____

People I met today (good, bad, and unique):
_____
_____
_____

Food/activities:
_____
_____
_____

Favorite memory of today:
_____
_____
_____

I'd like to forget about:
_____
_____
_____

Daily Travel Journal

Today's Date _____
The weather was _____

I woke up ... (where? When? Anything notable?) _____
_____

I went to bed ... (where? When? Anything notable?) _____
_____

Today's transportation included: walking car bus train plane bike boat
other: _____

People I met today (good, bad, and unique):
_____
_____

Food/activities:
_____
_____

Favorite memory of today:
_____
_____

I'd like to forget about:
_____
_____
_____

TRAVEL TALES & TIPS

Daily Travel Journal

Today's Date _____
The weather was _____

I woke up ... (where? When? Anything notable?) _____
_____

I went to bed ... (where? When? Anything notable?) _____
_____

Today's transportation included: walking car bus train plane bike boat
other: _____
_____

People I met today (good, bad, and unique):
_____
_____
_____

Food/activities:
_____
_____
_____

Favorite memory of today:
_____
_____
_____

I'd like to forget about:
_____
_____
_____

Daily Travel Journal

Today's Date _____

The weather was _____

I woke up ... (where? When? Anything notable?) _____
_____

I went to bed ... (where? When? Anything notable?) _____
_____

Today's transportation included: walking car bus train plane bike boat other: _____
_____

People I met today (good, bad, and unique):
_____
_____
_____

Food/activities:
_____
_____
_____

Favorite memory of today:
_____
_____
_____

I'd like to forget about:
_____
_____
_____

TRAVEL TALES & TIPS

Daily Travel Journal

Today's Date _____

The weather was _____

I woke up ... (where? When? Anything notable?) _____
_____

I went to bed ... (where? When? Anything notable?) _____
_____

Today's transportation included: walking car bus train plane bike boat other: _____
_____

People I met today (good, bad, and unique):
_____
_____
_____

Food/activities:
_____
_____
_____

Favorite memory of today:
_____
_____
_____

I'd like to forget about:
_____
_____
_____

Daily Travel Journal

Today's Date _____

The weather was _____

I woke up ... (where? When? Anything notable?) _____
_____

I went to bed ... (where? When? Anything notable?) _____
_____

Today's transportation included: walking car bus train plane bike boat other: _____
_____

People I met today (good, bad, and unique):
_____
_____
_____

Food/activities:
_____
_____
_____

Favorite memory of today:
_____
_____
_____

I'd like to forget about:
_____
_____
_____

TRAVEL TALES & TIPS

Daily Travel Journal

Today's Date _____
The weather was _____

I woke up ... (where? When? Anything notable?) _____
_____

I went to bed ... (where? When? Anything notable?) _____
_____

Today's transportation included: walking car bus train plane bike boat other: _____
_____

People I met today (good, bad, and unique):
_____
_____
_____

Food/activities:
_____
_____
_____

Favorite memory of today:
_____
_____
_____

I'd like to forget about:
_____
_____
_____

Daily Travel Journal

Today's Date _____
The weather was _____

I woke up ... (where? When? Anything notable?) _____
_____

I went to bed ... (where? When? Anything notable?) _____
_____

Today's transportation included: walking car bus train plane bike boat other: _____
_____

People I met today (good, bad, and unique):
_____
_____
_____

Food/activities:
_____
_____
_____

Favorite memory of today:
_____
_____
_____

I'd like to forget about:
_____
_____
_____

TRAVEL TALES & TIPS

Daily Travel Journal

Today's Date _____
The weather was _____

I woke up ... (where? When? Anything notable?) _____
_____

I went to bed ... (where? When? Anything notable?) _____
_____

Today's transportation included: walking car bus train plane bike boat other: _____

People I met today (good, bad, and unique):
_____
_____
_____

Food/activities:
_____
_____
_____

Favorite memory of today:
_____
_____
_____

I'd like to forget about:
_____
_____
_____

Daily Travel Journal

Today's Date _____
The weather was _____

I woke up ... (where? When? Anything notable?) _____
_____

I went to bed ... (where? When? Anything notable?) _____
_____

Today's transportation included: walking car bus train plane bike boat other: _____
_____

People I met today (good, bad, and unique):
_____
_____
_____

Food/activities:
_____
_____
_____

Favorite memory of today:
_____
_____
_____

I'd like to forget about:
_____
_____
_____

TRAVEL TALES & TIPS

Daily Travel Journal

Today's Date _____
The weather was _____

I woke up ... (where? When? Anything notable?) _____
_____

I went to bed ... (where? When? Anything notable?) _____
_____

Today's transportation included: walking car bus train plane bike boat other: _____
_____

People I met today (good, bad, and unique):
_____
_____
_____

Food/activities:
_____
_____
_____

Favorite memory of today:
_____
_____
_____

I'd like to forget about:
_____
_____
_____

Daily Travel Journal

Today's Date _____
The weather was _____

I woke up ... (where? When? Anything notable?) _____
_____

I went to bed ... (where? When? Anything notable?) _____
_____

Today's transportation included: walking car bus train plane bike boat other: _____
_____

People I met today (good, bad, and unique):
_____
_____
_____

Food/activities:
_____
_____
_____

Favorite memory of today:
_____
_____
_____

I'd like to forget about:
_____
_____
_____

TRAVEL TALES & TIPS

Daily Travel Journal

Today's Date _____

The weather was _____

I woke up ... (where? When? Anything notable?) _____
_____

I went to bed ... (where? When? Anything notable?) _____
_____

Today's transportation included: walking car bus train plane bike boat other: _____
_____

People I met today (good, bad, and unique):
_____
_____
_____

Food/activities:
_____
_____
_____

Favorite memory of today:
_____
_____
_____

I'd like to forget about:
_____
_____
_____

Daily Travel Journal

Today's Date _____
The weather was _____

I woke up ... (where? When? Anything notable?) _____
_____

I went to bed ... (where? When? Anything notable?) _____
_____

Today's transportation included: walking car bus train plane bike boat other: _____
_____

People I met today (good, bad, and unique):
_____
_____
_____

Food/activities:
_____
_____
_____

Favorite memory of today:
_____
_____

I'd like to forget about:
_____
_____
_____

TRAVEL TALES & TIPS

Daily Travel Journal

Today's Date _____

The weather was _____

I woke up ... (where? When? Anything notable?) _____
_____

I went to bed ... (where? When? Anything notable?) _____
_____

Today's transportation included: walking car bus train plane bike boat other: _____
_____

People I met today (good, bad, and unique):
_____
_____
_____

Food/activities:
_____
_____
_____

Favorite memory of today:
_____
_____
_____

I'd like to forget about:
_____
_____
_____

Daily Travel Journal

Today's Date _____
The weather was _____

I woke up ... (where? When? Anything notable?) _____
_____

I went to bed ... (where? When? Anything notable?) _____
_____

Today's transportation included: walking car bus train plane bike boat other: _____
_____

People I met today (good, bad, and unique):
_____
_____
_____

Food/activities:
_____
_____
_____

Favorite memory of today:
_____
_____
_____

I'd like to forget about:
_____
_____
_____

TRAVEL TALES & TIPS

Daily Travel Journal

Today's Date _____

The weather was _____

I woke up ... (where? When? Anything notable?) _____
_____

I went to bed ... (where? When? Anything notable?) _____
_____

Today's transportation included: walking car bus train plane bike boat other: _____
_____

People I met today (good, bad, and unique):
_____
_____
_____

Food/activities:
_____
_____
_____

Favorite memory of today:
_____
_____
_____

I'd like to forget about:
_____
_____
_____

Daily Travel Journal

Today's Date _____
The weather was _____

I woke up ... (where? When? Anything notable?) _____
_____

I went to bed ... (where? When? Anything notable?) _____
_____

Today's transportation included: walking car bus train plane bike boat other: _____
_____

People I met today (good, bad, and unique):
_____
_____
_____

Food/activities:
_____
_____
_____

Favorite memory of today:
_____
_____
_____

I'd like to forget about:
_____
_____
_____

TRAVEL TALES & TIPS

Daily Travel Journal

Today's Date _____

The weather was _____

I woke up ... (where? When? Anything notable?) _____
_____

I went to bed ... (where? When? Anything notable?) _____
_____

Today's transportation included: walking car bus train plane bike boat other: _____

People I met today (good, bad, and unique):
_____
_____
_____

Food/activities:
_____
_____
_____

Favorite memory of today:
_____
_____
_____

I'd like to forget about:
_____
_____
_____

Daily Travel Journal

Today's Date _____
The weather was _____

I woke up ... (where? When? Anything notable?) _____
_____

I went to bed ... (where? When? Anything notable?) _____
_____

Today's transportation included: walking car bus train plane bike boat other: _____
_____

People I met today (good, bad, and unique):
_____
_____
_____

Food/activities:
_____
_____
_____

Favorite memory of today:
_____
_____
_____

I'd like to forget about:
_____
_____
_____

TRAVEL TALES & TIPS

Daily Travel Journal

Today's Date _____
The weather was _____

I woke up ... (where? When? Anything notable?) _____
_____

I went to bed ... (where? When? Anything notable?) _____
_____

Today's transportation included: walking car bus train plane bike boat
other: _____

People I met today (good, bad, and unique):
_____
_____
_____

Food/activities:
_____
_____
_____

Favorite memory of today:
_____
_____
_____

I'd like to forget about:
_____
_____
_____

Daily Travel Journal

Today's Date _____

The weather was _____

I woke up ... (where? When? Anything notable?) _____
_____

I went to bed ... (where? When? Anything notable?) _____
_____

Today's transportation included: walking car bus train plane bike boat other: _____
_____

People I met today (good, bad, and unique):
_____
_____
_____

Food/activities:
_____
_____
_____

Favorite memory of today:
_____
_____
_____

I'd like to forget about:
_____
_____
_____

TRAVEL TALES & TIPS

Daily Travel Journal

Today's Date _____
The weather was _____

I woke up ... (where? When? Anything notable?) _____
_____

I went to bed ... (where? When? Anything notable?) _____
_____

Today's transportation included: walking car bus train plane bike boat other: _____
_____

People I met today (good, bad, and unique):
_____
_____
_____

Food/activities:
_____
_____
_____

Favorite memory of today:
_____
_____
_____

I'd like to forget about:
_____
_____
_____

Daily Travel Journal

Today's Date _____
The weather was _____

I woke up ... (where? When? Anything notable?) _____
_____

I went to bed ... (where? When? Anything notable?) _____
_____

Today's transportation included: walking car bus train plane bike boat other: _____

People I met today (good, bad, and unique):

Food/activities:

Favorite memory of today:

I'd like to forget about:

TRAVEL TALES & TIPS

Daily Travel Journal

Today's Date _____
The weather was _____

I woke up … (Where? When? Anything notable?) _____
_____

I went to bed … (Where? When? Anything notable?) _____
_____

Today's transportation included: walking car bus train plane bike boat other: _____
_____

People I met today (good, bad, and unique):
_____
_____
_____

Food/activities:
_____
_____
_____

Favorite memory of today:
_____
_____
_____

I'd like to forget about:
_____
_____
_____

Daily Travel Journal

Today's Date _____
The weather was _____

I woke up ... (where? When? Anything notable?) _____
_____

I went to bed ... (where? When? Anything notable?) _____
_____

Today's transportation included: walking car bus train plane bike boat other: _____
_____

People I met today (good, bad, and unique):
_____
_____
_____

Food/activities:
_____
_____
_____

Favorite memory of today:
_____
_____
_____

I'd like to forget about:
_____
_____
_____

TRAVEL TALES & TIPS

Daily Travel Journal

Today's Date _____
The weather was _____

I woke up ... (where? When? Anything notable?) _____
_____

I went to bed ... (where? When? Anything notable?) _____
_____

Today's transportation included: walking car bus train plane bike boat
other: _____

People I met today (good, bad, and unique):
_____
_____
_____

Food/activities:
_____
_____
_____

Favorite memory of today:
_____
_____
_____

I'd like to forget about:
_____
_____
_____

Daily Travel Journal

Today's Date _____

The weather was _____

I woke up ... (where? When? Anything notable?) _____
_____

I went to bed ... (where? When? Anything notable?) _____
_____

Today's transportation included: walking car bus train plane bike boat other: _____

People I met today (good, bad, and unique):
_____
_____
_____

Food/activities:
_____
_____
_____

Favorite memory of today:
_____
_____
_____

I'd like to forget about:
_____
_____
_____

TRAVEL TALES & TIPS

Daily Travel Journal

Today's Date _____
The weather was _____

I woke up ... (where? When? Anything notable?) _____
_____

I went to bed ... (where? When? Anything notable?) _____
_____

Today's transportation included: walking car bus train plane bike boat
other: _____
_____

People I met today (good, bad, and unique):
_____
_____
_____

Food/activities:
_____
_____
_____

Favorite memory of today:
_____
_____
_____

I'd like to forget about:
_____
_____
_____

Daily Travel Journal

Today's Date _____

The weather was _____

I woke up ... (where? When? Anything notable?) _____
_____

I went to bed ... (where? When? Anything notable?) _____
_____

Today's transportation included: walking car bus train plane bike boat other: _____
_____

People I met today (good, bad, and unique):
_____
_____
_____

Food/activities:
_____
_____
_____

Favorite memory of today:
_____
_____
_____

I'd like to forget about:
_____
_____
_____

Meet Our Contributors

Lynn Aloia is a lifelong traveler. Her love for traveling started when her mother took her on a cross-country bus trip at the age of five.

She is a proud United States Navy Veteran who served in the field of communications. Her last duty station was in Spain. She requested her honorable discharge be issued locally so she could travel abroad. This gave her the opportunity to backpack 13 European and U.K. countries with her then fiancé, now husband, before returning to the United States. She has traveled to thirty-five countries on five continents and plans to keep increasing that number.

Her love for travel, quest for knowledge and her "there is no limit to what one can accomplish" attitude has helped to propel her through life.

She is a constant learner and holds a multitude of degrees and certificates in diverse areas including a BFA in communications from NYIT and a sports, entertainment, and event marketing certificate from NYU. She also holds a degree in business administration and is a trained travel agent and certified tour guide.

Her career includes experience in radio, television, music, modeling, public relations, marketing, and so much more.

In 1995, Lynn launched her own business, Everything's Planned, dedicated to the planning and management of meetings and events, mostly in the entertainment industry.

In 2012 she began the networking group, The Inside Connection, connecting people in the entertainment, media, performing arts, fashion, and other creative professionals.

Lynn contributes to various Long Island non-profit organizations through partnerships and volunteering.

Her hobbies include reading, listening to music, trying new things, and seeing the world. Her section of this book includes insights gained from her own experiences and adventures.

Originally from West Virginia, she currently splits her time between New York and Florida, with her husband, Joe, and their fur-kitty babies Jax and Thor.

Robert Intelisano is a world traveler who has touched foot on all 7 continents. He became obsessed with travel and frequent flyer points since 1991 when he was promoted to a Manager by Prudential Insurance and relocated from New York City to upstate Buffalo New York. While he was looking for housing, Prudential was paying to fly him from JFK to Buffalo round trip every week. The distance is 305 miles (350 points at 1 point per mile). US Air had a rule that the "minimum segment" on any trip was 750 points; hence, Robert received 1500 points per week paid for by Prudential as companies didn't use points back then.

Robert combines travel with his passion for family, sports, music, pizza, writing, racing, risk taking and men's fashion to name a few. An accomplished writer, Robert wrote a newspaper column called "The Financial Wave" during Covid-19 which started as "weekly Covid briefings" for his clients. He has also led 20 pizza crawls and has found outstanding pizza all over the world, such as "The Sicilian" in Parramatta, Australia and "Lupita" in Lisbon, Portugal.

"Just say yes," especially when it involves travel is Robert' biggest tip! His 2009 Africa trip as a "stand-in" for an injured friend gave him his first "Travel High" that he needed more of. His Top 3 Trips are 1. Antarctica (With Quark Travel) 2. Africa (Jaci's Tree Lodge in Botswana) and 3. Australia (Great Barrier Reef). Bon Voyage!!!

Stephanie Larkin is the "head penguin" of Red Penguin Books an independent publishing company working with authors from around the world of all types and genres. She is the author of several books on writing and publishing, and the ghostwriter of many non-fiction books. Stephanie is the host of television's *The Author Corner*, an award-winning educational cable TV series airing in Queens and Long Island, airing on Verizon and Optimum, and on podcast platforms worldwide. Her goal and company motto is "Changing lives ... one book at a time!"

When she isn't publishing books, Stephanie and her globetrotting family enjoy everything from cruising to ballooning, hiking to diving, and everything in between. She has been to 50 states and 32 countries, with many more on her horizon, if only to catch up her to well-traveled kids.

Janet Lipkin Bein is a retired Silicon Valley technical writer who loves to write and to travel. She has published articles (under Janet Bein) about her travel adventures in Peru, Ecuador, Guatemala, Mexico. and Argentina, and locations closer to home. You can find her articles in the online magazine, www.tangodiva.com.

Wandering troubadour Lorraine Caputo is a documentary poet, translator and travel writer. Her works appear internationally in over 500 journals and 24 collections of poetry – including In the Jaguar Valley (dancing girl press, 2023) and Santa Marta Ayres (Origami Poems Project, 2024). She also authors travel narratives, articles and guidebooks. She is a Parliamentary Poet Laureate of Canada honoree (2011), and Best of the Net and Pushcart Prize nominee. Caputo has taken over 100 trains between Alaska and the Patagonia. She journeys through Latin America with her faithful knapsack Rocinante, listening to the voices of the pueblos and Earth. Follow her travels at: https://latinamericawanderer.wordpress.com.

Carolyn Donnell has been published in anthologies and won awards in fiction, poetry, and memoir from San Francisco Writers Conference, San Mateo County Fair Literary Arts, and more. Also two novels (under C. S. Donnell). CWC South Bay's 2018

Matthews-Baldwin service award and CWC's 2019 Jack London Award.

https://www.amazon.com/C-S-Donnell/e/B017GGDZTI

https://carolyndonnell.wordpress.com

Joseph A. Farina is a retired lawyer in Sarnia, Ontario, Canada. An award winning,push cart nominee, internatianally published poet , his works published in many poetry magazines notably Quills Canadian Poetry Magazine, The Windsor Review, and appears in the anthologies *Sweet Lemons: Writings with a Sicilian Accent*, *Canadian Italians at Table*, *Witness* and *Tamaracks: Canadian Poetry for the 21st Century*. He has had two books of poetry published— *The Cancer Chronicles* and *The Ghosts of Water Street* and an E-book *Sunsets in Black and White*.and his latest book, *The beach, the street and everything in between*.

Gayle Lauradunn has travelled to over 40 countries, and always looks for landscape, history, and how other cultures differ from ours. Her fourth poetry collection CONSIDER THIS is now available from Kelsay Books, local bookstores, and Amazon.

Matt McGee writes in the Los Angeles area. His story 'Sins of the Father' appeared in Red Penguin's collection 'Trick or Treat.' In 2024 his work has appeared in Spectrum, Gnashing Teeth, The NonBinary Review and others. When not typing he drives around in rented cars and plays goalie in local hockey leagues.

Terry A. Repak is the author of a travel memoir, "Circling Home: What I Learned By Living Elsewhere," and two other nonfiction books as well as articles and short stories. Zanzibar and Tanzania were the favorite places where Terry has lived and traveled. You can find more on Substack at https://terryrepak.substack.com/ as well as at https://www.terryrepak.com/.

William John Rostron is best known for his "Band in the Wind" series, a four-book saga rooted in 1960s American culture and music. Born and raised in Queens, New York, he now divides his time between his Long Island residence and traveling across the United States in a Tiffin motorhome with his wife, Marilyn. Over the past two decades, they've journeyed through all 50 states, visited every Major League Baseball stadium, and explored over 100 national parks, experiences that often inspire the settings in his writings.

Jasmine Tritten is an award-winning author, photographer and artist born in Denmark. She has been journaling since childhood and traveled extensively. Her numerous short stories have been published in various anthologies. Jasmine has published two books and co-authored four others. All her books contain photos and original artwork. Her latest book "Around the World in 80 Years," she wrote with her husband with whom she resides in New Mexico together with an ever-changing number of cats.

After teaching Russian and English at schools, colleges and universities, Larisa Veselova moved to the USA to join her daughter's family and started to write memoirs and stories about families. This essay is about her childhood.

Janet Metz Walter's first book for Red Penguin was an anthology of real stories called 'The 2 Carrot Ring and Other Fascinating Jewelry Stories." She does interactive programs with organizations where participants tell their own personal jewelry stories. She is also a mentor to beginning authors, and a book reviewer, as well as a teacher of the game of Mah Jongg among the several other positions she has held.

As a former travel agent she was thrilled to be able to travel the world and all 50 states with her husband and two children, partially using her "Unexpected Gift." There were special things about every place she traveled to but at the moment her favorite city in Europe is Barcelona because of all the fabulous architecture by Antoni Gaudi. She has contributed stories to seven anthologies including "London, Rome, and New York, and hopes to be able to share some more of her million stories of her experiences.

Also from the Red Penguin Travel Series

London: Smokes, Blokes, and Jokes of Foggy Town
Paris: Love, Loss and Longing in the City of Lights
Rome: Centuries of Stories of the Eternal City

www.ingramcontent.com/pod-product-compliance
Lightning Source LLC
Chambersburg PA
CBHW061747070526
44585CB00025B/2817